❧

GUARDIAN ANGELS ALONG MY HOMELESS PATH

❧ ❧ ❧

Ulyses B. Hooks Jr. and Narayan Persaud, PhD.

Bloomington, IN Milton Keynes, UK

authorHOUSE™

AuthorHouse™
1663 Liberty Drive, Suite 200
Bloomington, IN 47403
www.authorhouse.com
Phone: 1-800-839-8640

AuthorHouse™ *UK Ltd.*
500 Avebury Boulevard
Central Milton Keynes, MK9 2BE
www.authorhouse.co.uk
Phone: 08001974150

This book is a work of non-fiction. Unless otherwise noted, the author and the publisher make no explicit guarantees as to the accuracy of the information contained in this book and in some cases, names of people and places have been altered to protect their privacy.

First published by AuthorHouse 4/18/2006

ISBN: 1-4259-2537-5 (sc)

Printed in the United States of America
Bloomington, Indiana

This book is printed on acid-free paper.

DEDICATION

To my daughter Aria Hooks who lives in my very Soul.
And to the many Guardian Angels who assisted me as I
wandered aimlessly along the Homeless Path

CONTENTS

ACKNOWLEDGEMENT

Over the years, as I traveled the homeless path, I was lucky to meet many beautiful people who never gave up on me. Without them, this book would not have been possible. To them I owe thanks.

Special thanks to Dr. Narayan Persaud whose patience I tested to the limit; but, he stood by me so that I could realize my dream of completing this book. Thanks also to the ladies at the Florida A & M Coleman library, Cornelia Taylor, Joyce Johnson, Barbara Proctor, Faye Williams, Priscilla Henry, Brenda Wright, Carolyn Graham and Carla Harrison, all of whom were gracious in their support. Over the years they have become my friends. Special thanks also to Emmit Hunt, the Reverend Ivy Williams and Gerri Chambers; they also stood by me in my times of need.

I would also like to give special thanks to my sister Julie who never lost contact with me; she always kept money on the pre-paid phone card I carried around. Thanks sis for keeping me linked to your world, and making it possible for me to keep in contact with a few others in the family.

In my early days of drifting, my brother Craig and his wife Francois were my pillars, and to them I owe my gratitude.

And, to my mom Helen Hooks; even though we have had a rocky relationship, she shared some of my pains.

CHAPTER 1
One Day of Life

Some times at the peak of a very pleasant afternoon with friends, my gaiety would come to an abrupt end at the realization that I must catch the last bus back to the homeless shelter. Almost always, I would hurriedly pack my backpack and rush through the door with this painful reality in mind: *The shelter has become my home; a respite for my tired fifty eight year old body that weakened gradually over the years as a result of personal neglect and abuse.* On occasions, in my haste to be on time for the bus, I would forget to bid my friends farewell. Without fail, Ms. Perkins would call out after me, "Ulyses, what happened? Where are you going?" "Nothing, Ms. Perkins," I would reply, "Just that I am late for my bus to the shelter." Ms. Perkins, a dark skinned compassionate African American woman was always the last to leave the classroom building which housed her office and that of my professor.

Each day, from Monday through Friday, I would go to my professor's office at seven thirty, brew a pot of coffee and spend time reading criminological and social science literature. Almost daily, a student or two would stop by the office to chat, or ask about lost and found because they misplaced their keys, cell phones or book bags in the building. During these encounters, I would engage students in conversations, encouraging them to work hard and excel. Using my own life as an example, I would impress upon them the consequences of misguidance, youthful extravagance and missed opportunities. I can't say for sure whether they heeded or cared about my advise, but I offered them anyway.

As part of my day's activities I would run errands for Dr. P and Dr. Dix. Most often, I would drop off or pick up exams at the copy center. Walking back and forth to the center, I frequently stopped by the library to visit for a few minutes with the staff, several of whom I have come to know over the years. I would also stop to say hello to Chris. During his class breaks, Chris regularly stood outside of the classroom building smoking cigarettes, and chatting with other students. A stocky, soft spoken, courteous Jamaican student with dreadlocks, Chris is well known for his affable personality and pleasant demeanor. His warm smile and soft hello regularly serve to brighten my day. If not pressed for time, Chris and I would share cigarettes and talk about the issues of the day. Customarily, I would start out by asking, "Chris have you seen the newspaper today?" And, without waiting for his reply I would engage him in conversation on various subjects. At the end of these conversations, Chris would politely say in his Jamaican accent, "See you layta Ulyses, gat to go to class now."

Taking breaks from my daily reading, Ms. Perkins and I would go outside the building to smoke cigarettes and chat. Serving as the Internship Director for the department of Sociology and Criminal Justice, Ms. Perkins has assisted numerous students in obtaining work experience and securing employment upon graduation. Some of her former students have become Federal Marshals, while others work for various Federal, State and Local government agencies. Because of the relationship Ms. Perkins and I have developed over the years, she seemed to forget that I was homeless, and that the shelter has become my "home". It was out of such mindset that she would call out, "Ulyses what happened? Where are you going?" Then, upon recollecting her thoughts her expression would change. It seemed as if realization often stepped in to remind her that my haste to catch the bus was timed to *the closing of the homeless shelter.*

❦

CHAPTER 2
My Early Years

My life of homelessness did not occur overnight. It resulted from years of constant struggle, mishaps, and misfortunes. Like most newborn infants, I came into the world kicking and screaming on July 21, 1947 in Oklahoma City, Oklahoma. My father, Ulyses Sr., a Navy veteran and a tailor by trade, worked as a bellhop and waiter. As far as I can recall, I didn't see him much during my early years. Like most men of his time, dad had to work long hours to provide for his family. He left for work early in the mornings while we were still asleep, and returned late in the evenings when we had gone to bed. In our little minds such was the life of most dads.

On occasions we did see dad during the day, but this was primarily because Ma had phoned him to come home and discipline one or all of us. Upon his arrival home, my mother would rattle off our misbehaviors with impeccable recall and fluency. Her complaints regularly served to prime dad's anger and energize him into action. Grabbing us by the arm, he would proceed to whip us with whatever he could lay his hands on, a belt, a coat hanger or anything usable. Immediately after a whipping, our good behavior would somehow return, only to disappear as soon as the stinging from the lashes eased. There was no telling how long it took for good behavior to end and bad behavior to resume. Some times the stinging would last from an hour to several days depending on the intensity of dad's wrath for having to leave work on account of our misbehaviors. Still vivid in my mind today is one stinging that lasted for several days. It happened when I was about age nine.

As a habit, dad left the tips he earned at work in a night stand drawer by his bed. Knowing that he regularly left his bedroom door open, I would sneak in and grab a handful of money during his absence. To avoid suspicion, I would hide the loot in the pockets of my pants I had prepared to wear to school that day. Once, I happened to grab a fifty dollar bill that was among the money dad had left in the drawer. Because it was a large bill, dad realized it was gone shortly after I swiped it. Without suspecting any of the children, he accused my mother of taking the fifty dollar bill. Knowing that she didn't take the money, mom decided to investigate. By the process of elimination, she quickly deduced that I had taken the money. She spared no time in informing my dad who then proceeded to give me such a trashing, the pains lasted for several days. To add insult to my bodily pains, dad refused to let me eat dinner at the table with the rest of the family. "This family does not want to eat dinner with a thief," he said to me. The statement tore my little heart, not because I fully grasped the meaning, but because of the harshness in my father's voice. In addition, the ostracism I suffered from the family, though of short duration, made me hate everything at least for a while.

Now, whenever I reflect on the incident, I would smile for I can clearly see my own mischievousness. But, things were not always this way. The discomforts from the whipping, and the humiliation from being excluded at the dinner table, lingered within me for a long time afterwards, planting seeds of bitterness and resentment.

In being a strict disciplinarian dad felt he was preparing his children to face the harsh realities of adult life. From the things he said, I gathered that he acquired his sense of discipline while serving in the Navy. Being amongst the Navy's first draftees, he boasted regularly about severing his country with honor and pride.

The sense of responsibility my dad acquired from his military training, he carried over to his job and his family. He worked long hours and took pride in whatever he did to earn his income. As his way of inculcating in us a sense of responsibility, he called on us each weekend to assist him in taking care of the yard. I can't remember if we did anything much but it felt like we never took breaks. Whatever we did, we worked at it until our little bodies ached. To all of us, dad acted as if he was the army general and we were his little troopers.

Much like my father, my mother was also a disciplinarian but with a different twist. Instead of whipping us with anything she could lay her hands on, she would send someone to fetch a switch from a tree in the back yard. This she used on us with much dexterity but with less severity than dad.

And, as soon as the switching ended, we reverted quickly to being little rascals.

Despite being a disciplinarian, my mother regularly bestowed us with affection. She took pride in being a mother and housewife. And, when the demands of motherhood lessened, she sought and gained employment as a scrub technician at the neighborhood hospital. To me, Ma didn't display the same work ethic as Dad. Yet, she managed to keep her job for as long as she desired.

During my early childhood, we lived in several places, first at a housing project the government had established in Edward's Park for military veterans. We then moved to my paternal grandparents' house and finally our own home. At the Park, life was a bundle of fun and frolic. Even though we lived there for only a year, I can still recall the beauty of the housing units. Stacked neatly in rows, the units were distant enough to provide space for pathways. These pathways, and the empty space on the outskirts of the Park, became our haven. No sooner had we moved into one of the units, we made friends with some of the children who lived in the park. It seemed as if we became one big happy noisy family almost instantly. The taunts, the jeers and the innocence that accompanied our daily play often resulted in joyous screams and laughter. Now and then, however, someone would become upset and a scuffle would ensue. Afraid to let our parents know about our occasional fights, we would quickly try to resolve the disputes among ourselves.

During the time we lived in the park, my brother and I developed a close relationship. Although only a year my senior, my brother acted as my protector. I looked up to him and abided by his wishes. Each time I fought or found myself in difficulties with the other children, my brother would step in to defend me. Some times he, in his efforts to defend me, ended up in fist fights. And, since he defeated most of the opponents, my admiration for him grew stronger with each victory. Soon, as a result of my brother's reputation as a 'tough guy', I became known as Little Hooks. To be honest, I relished the new title for it kept the bullies away from me and made me feel untouchable.

Daily life for the children in Edwards Park didn't vary much, a set of made-up games, foot-racing and several trips to the nearby playground took up most of our time. While I can't recall the details of my early life, one incident sticks out in my mind. It happened the day my father's younger brother paid us a visit. Dad had already left for work, but for some unknown reason did not take his car. Seeing the car at home, my uncle decided to drive to the nearby store. As he was about to leave, I pleaded with him to take me along but he refused. I recall going out of the door and walking to the back of the car. Using the height of the car as my shield, I stood in a manner so that I would not be readily seen.

My uncle came out of the house and without paying much attention, got into the car and started to drive away. Instinctively, I grabbed on to the back bumper believing I could ride along this way. Traveling down the Park's dirt road, the car moved slowly. I ran as fast as I could, keeping my grip on the bumper. When my uncle reached the paved road outside the Park, he began to travel a little faster. My little feet buckled, unable to run as fast as the car was moving. Yet, I held on to the bumper.

Drivers in their passing vehicles saw me hanging on to the car. They honked their horns and pointed towards me, signaling to my uncle that something was amiss. My uncle stopped, and walked to the back of the car to investigate. There, he discovered me hanging on to the bumper with my feet torn to bits. Immediately, he became extremely angry but did not say anything. Instead, he put me in the car, got me some ice cream, and then took me home. I don't recall how long my feet took to heal, or what my parents said at the time, only that I cried for a long time after being taken home.

CHAPTER 3
Schooling: My Early Years

In 1952, I entered kindergarten. School gave me my first opportunity to meet and establish social contacts with children other than my cousins and neighborhood friends. Kindergarten proved to be a new experience for me. Besides being in the company of children I had never seen before, I had to abide by a new set of rules, and share things with my classmates. To be quite honest, I was reluctant to share with children I did not know. In my mind, many did not want to share with me either. However, as the days passed, I gradually learned to accept and share with the other children in my class. Before long, they too shared with me. In the process of such exchanges, I made a few new friends but never got too close to any of them. Since I had my older brother around, I felt I didn't need anyone else to keep me company. As a matter of fact, the relationship between my brother and I strengthened as we grew older. With each passing day, we became better friends.

By the time I was seven, we had moved into our own three bedroom home in a newly established section of town called Garden Oaks. My brother and I were quite excited since it meant we would have the opportunity to share a bedroom. Prior to moving into our new home, we lived for a while in my paternal grandparents' house since our home was still under construction. As soon as we found out that the house would be ready for us to move into, my brother and I began to pack our meager belongings in anticipation of the move. During the first week at the new house, we stayed up late into the nights talking excitedly about everything but nothing in particular. We were happy. Our new home felt like paradise. Weeks passed before we began to explore our new neighborhood. Dad kept a close watch over us, and we quickly learned not to be out of ear shot of his whistle. Whistling was his way to summon us back home, and failure to hear the signal meant punishment. Knowing that we must be alert to dad's whistling call, my brother and I visited only those friends who lived a few houses away from us.

Residing in Garden Oaks, our family gradually grew. To me, it did not take long for us to become four sisters and four brothers, me, included. The demanding youngsters soon caused my brother and I to become parental assistants. Being the two eldest children, we were constantly called upon to assist with taking care of the younger ones. For many years my brother and I changed diapers, combed and braided the hair of our younger siblings. Though children ourselves, assisting with the care and protection of our younger siblings became a part of our everyday reality, a fact of daily life. These adult responsibilities, on occasions, altered my own childhood experiences. One that I still remember vividly is missing my junior prom because I had to baby-sit. I had anxiously awaited the event with much anticipation of being dressed up and hanging out with my classmates for the last time. It didn't happen. My parents deemed my baby sitting responsibilities to be more important than my attendance to this once in a life time childhood event.

⅜ ⅜ ⅜

Today, whenever I phone my younger brothers and sisters, images of their childhood would flow through my mind, often bringing tears to my eyes. They were too young to remember the assistance they received from my older brother and me. Even if they try to recall some things, it does not really matter any more. It is over a decade now since I have seen some of them. Despite being grown men and women, in my mind's eye I still seem to see them as my little brothers and sisters. I have not seen them for some years now. If we happen to have a chance encounter, would they recognize me, or me, them? Just thinking of this question saddens me for I do miss them. The memories of childhood can be razor sharp at times, cutting into ones consciousness with a surgeon's precision, only to reveal the repressed memories and hidden emotions of a distant past. My distant past is my present day reality.

⅜ ⅜ ⅜

From 1953 to 1958, I attended the elementary school in my neighborhood. School provided some relief from my baby-sitting chores and opened up a whole new world for me. I loved school and soon became intrigued with learning new things. Each day, I dressed hurriedly and rushed on my way to school in anticipation of discovering something new. I do not know the source of my educational inspiration only that I admired some of my teachers; Ms. Johnson being the best. Ms. Johnson, a stately woman, loved her students and took great pains in instructing them. Within a few days at school, I became fascinated with Ms. Johnson. She made me realize that I could be loved by someone other than my family. Ms. Johnson treated her students with much love and devotion. Her encouragement and support increased my eagerness to learn. She made me feel that she would be personally disappointed if I failed. Some times, in my current state, I would reflect back on Ms. Johnson and wonder what has become of her. Perhaps she was the first *Guardian Angel* in my path. She opened up my little heart and mind, and instilled in me the love of reading. It was she who made me believe that learning can be exciting.

Besides academics, grade school provided me the opportunity to participate in extra curricular activities. From the inception, my involvement in organized school activities made me feel special. I knew I performed better than most of my class mates even though I felt somewhat detached from them. Participating in organized activities enabled me to break out of my shell and become a part of the group. I am not sure of how I came to participate in the organized activities since I lacked both skills and confidence. This became clear to me while I was in the third grade. Somehow, I became a member of the singing group. I knew then that I couldn't hold a musical note even if my life depended on it. Yet, I became a member of the group. To cover up my ineptitude, I would lip sync. Whether my teacher knew of my fakery, I am unsure. Perhaps she knew but she neither said anything, nor dropped me from the group. And, when the group had an opportunity to sing at a radio station, she took me along with the rest of the students. The humorous part of this experience came after we listened to ourselves on the radio. While the other children excitedly tried to isolate their own voices, I could not do the same; I knew I didn't utter a sound. This may sound funny; the one thing I couldn't fake was identifying my voice from that of others in the group. It simply was non existent.

My greatest excitement in grade school came while I was in the fifth grade. Because of my good academic performance, and my quiet disposition, my teacher selected me to be a member of the Junior Police. The Kiwanas Club, the sponsors of the Junior Police, gave me a white badge which I wore as a mark of distinction. Each day, I monitored the school's hallways and guided students across the street with enormous pride. I felt like a little emperor. The responsibilities of Junior Police played out happily in my daydreams. "Boy," I would silently say to myself, "me Ulyses B. Hooks is now a Junior Police, wow!"

As my young mind wandered about in elation, I would smile to myself. At times my silent reasoning became so warped it caused me to believe that my teacher chose me because of my name "Junior." From my point of view, my reasoning did not seem so far fetched since my real name is Ulyses B. Hooks Jr. Now that I am older, I would still smile whenever I recall my days as a Junior Police. I would smile, not because of the happy memories of being a Junior Police, but because of the recollection of my childhood innocence.

Being chosen as a Junior Police had nothing to do with the fact that my nickname was Junior. But, how was I to know? The young mind seems to reason and conjure up images that in adulthood one regularly find humorous. What an impact aging has had on my mind, my perception, and even my Spirit! The naiveté of my childhood haunts and taunts my aging Soul.

A few weeks after proudly carrying out my responsibilities as a Junior Police, the principal called me into the school's main office and abruptly took away my badge. Tearfully, I walked out of the office with my head hung in sadness. I cannot recall looking at anyone, or seeing any faces, as I walked through the doors and out into the street headed for home. In taking away my badge, the principal explained that some friends reported that a classmate and I bullied our way into their home and intimidated them. They withheld from the principal the fact that it was they who had invited us to their home. When we arrived at the house, my friends slammed the front door shut just as we were about to enter. Believing that we could outsmart them, we scampered in through the back door. Afraid that their parents would find out about our visit and punish them, my friends decided to report to the principal that we had forcibly entered their home. After taking away my Junior Police badge, the principal whipped me on the back several times, and reprimanded me. Stripped of my monitoring responsibilities, I felt pained and humiliated for a long time.

Feeling demoralized for having my police badge taken away, I avoided the company of my classmates. For several days my despondency lingered. I felt like never attending school again, and distanced myself from family members.

Sensing the turbulence in my little mind, my mother somehow felt my pain. She shared my disappointment the best way a mother knows how, with encouraging words and warm embraces. On occasions, in my adult loneliness, whenever I recalled the loss of my Junior Police badge, I would have fleeting images of the pain on my mother's face as she silently commiserated with me, her dejected son. Strange as it may seem, my mother and I drifted apart as I grew older.

In 1959, I entered the seventh grade and began attending Webster Junior High School with my older brother. Webster, formally a school for white children, became integrated the previous year. Integration meant nothing to me. In fact, my young mind could care less whether or not the school was integrated. I didn't understand the hoopla nor comprehend the meaning or reasons for integration. Attending school with white children did not fill me with excitement or indifference. I knew we were physically different from white children. They kept their distances and we kept ours. They lived in their own neighborhoods and we lived in ours. They didn't play with us and we did not play with them. Why the sudden change among the elders of the town? Little did I realize then that it would take less than a year for me to experience firsthand what the elders in my community discussed in hushed tones.

The first day of classes at Webster Junior High started with a bang. I had done well in grade school and felt adequately prepared for the academic challenges ahead. For some reason, I felt that Junior High signaled my coming of age. Elementary school presented little challenge so I felt adequately prepared to move on to the next level. Furthermore, my teachers believed in me and this helped me to excel. In addition, I enjoyed learning new things and looked forward to the challenges of Junior High, making new friends and feeling sort of grown up.

Initially, I can't say I experienced discomforts as a result of integration. As a matter of fact, the white and black students in attendance hardly interacted with each other. I can't recall seeing blacks and whites together as a group other than during sports' activities. Customarily, they maintained separate groups and kept their social distances.

While integration and its intent meant nothing to me, intuitively I began to change as the new school year approached. At the time, the few white students remaining at the school disappeared as Webster Junior High was reconverted into an all Black school. It was then that the whispering conversations of racism among the elders within my community began to make some sense.

Attending Junior High resulted in increasing competition between my classmates and me. We competed for practically everything: academics, sports, arts, crafts and little girls. Not very good at playing any sport, I just stuck around and watched my friends play. For a while, I did well in my academic subjects and developed a love for reading. My interests, however, waned as I moved up a grade. I began making new friends who shared little interest in schooling. Gradually, my entire academic interests diminished. I was gradually pulled towards truancy and nonconformity, but did not realize it at the time. This realization dawned on me some three years ago when I began accompanying my professor to the public schools and community centers around Tallahassee.

ᕲᕲ ᕲᕲ ᕲᕲ

Under the auspices of the Juvenile Justice Role Model Development Program (JJRMDP), Florida A & M University trains students to become role models and mentors to disadvantaged at-risk youths. At least once every week, college students go out into the neighboring communities and schools to mentor troubled youths. My professor, who is also the director of the Program, regularly accompanies the mentors to the places where they serve. As his graduate assistant, he invited me to join him on his field visits. Accompanying him around, I encountered many youths who became disenchanted with their schooling. Curious to learn about their problems, I began talking to some of these disaffected youths. Several of them noted their disinterests in academic learning and their interests in doing what they referred to as "fun things" such as playing computer games and just "hanging with each other." I too wanted to do the "fun things" at their age, and as I drifted away from school, delinquency came calling. I am not sure how a youth is supposed to know that this shift is taking place. I didn't, and I am sure many of today's at-risk youth don't. In talking to the youths, it became clear that little effort is made to stem their drift away from academic learning. As teachers became increasingly overwhelmed by academic demands and behavioral problems in the classrooms, few policy makers and educational architects seem to pay any attention. As I wrestled with my thoughts, my own youthful past came back to haunt me.

ᕲᕲ ᕲᕲ ᕲᕲ

In 1961, I was promoted to the ninth grade and began attending Douglass Senior High School. Going to Douglas High made me feel proud. I took my academic work seriously, and for some time did quite well. Then, for some unexplained reason, during my second year, I began to drink alcohol and get into fistfights with other students. Hanging out with friends, drinking, and getting into trouble with school administrators, seemed to be "more cool" than mastering mathematical equations and reading the great literary works. Stepping foot on this path, I quickly lost all interest in academic learning. Without any guidance or counseling about employment, and lacking preparation for the realities of life after school, I became somewhat of a renegade. If my teachers or my parents tried to counsel me, I resisted their efforts. It is now obvious that I did not listen, or was not prepared to heed the advice of anyone. Youth, intertwined with ignorance, spelled doom, and I was doomed. In my mind, like some of the at-risk youths I encountered in the public school system, hanging with my friends and defying school administrators was "truly being cool." My intolerable behavior soon caught up with me and I was expelled for the rest of the 1963 academic year. If expulsion was meant to curb my deviant behavior, it failed. Instead, it pushed me further away from school and propelled me into ending my studentship at Douglass High.

CHAPTER 4
Growing Up A Hooks

The years of homelessness have taken a toll on my psyche and rent asunder my hopes of establishing a stable life. In times of despair, I would often think of my childhood community and the life I had back then. Tears would come to my eyes. The youth, the innocence have all vanished. What lingers, are the memories of things past. It is now clear to me that no matter how hard I try to distance myself from my past, the more it lives in my present. Stored in the core of my very Being are the memories of my youthful days gone by. And, while old age seems to have rushed in to take the place of youth, the memories of my innocent and naïve childhood linger, reminding me of the people, places and things that once played music to my soul. Though distanced by time, these memories come vividly to life in a manner that makes me feel that they were a part of my yesterday instead of my childhood past.

❧ ❧ ❧

I can still recall with some clarity when my family left the veterans housing project and moved to Edwards. Though not yet old enough to understand much, it was at Edwards that I began to experience a real sense of community. My parents moved there to take up residence in the home of my grandparents who had decided to return to Tatum, Oklahoma. Tatum, then, was a black town that my grandfather co-founded. Since my parents had purchased a new home that was still under construction, my grandparents agreed to let us live in their vacated home until ours was completed. Grandparents' home in Edwards had a front and back yard. To us, the young children, a front and backyard meant a life of fun and games. No sooner had we moved in, we skipped out into the yard exploring and making child's play, jumping, climbing, hiding, and doing what came naturally to young children at play – calling out loudly to each other to come over and take a look at the little things we discovered, the bugs, the birds, the discarded articles, the plants and animals.

In the backyard, my grandmother once raised chickens. There, she built a coop to house her brood. When we moved in, the chicken coop was still standing. Soon the coop became the center of me and my brother's fun and games. We climbed in, up, and around it, making up games to fit our fantasies. And, when these activities no longer held our interests, we went out into the alleyways located just behind the house. There we sat and chatted, or just laid on our backs and watched the clouds roll by in the sky. Some times, we took turns in picking a cloud and challenging each other to see the outlines of an animal in it. Thus, locked in the challenge of dueling imaginations, we felt free and unburdened.

Within a few months stay at my grandparents' home, my father announced the completion of our new home at The Garden Oaks. When we moved in, the streets in the community were still under construction. Being one of the first families to take up residence in The Garden Oaks community, my brother and I soon developed mixed feelings. We loved our new home, but missed the freedom of the outdoors my grandparents' home provided. Within a couple of months, however, we adjusted, and my brothers, sisters, and I gradually became integrated into the community. Soon, The Garden Oaks community became a place that symbolized the old African adage: *It takes a village to raise a child*. Every adult shouldered the responsibilities of parenting the community's children. You couldn't let them see you do anything wrong. If you did, they would not hesitate to punish you. To add salt to our wounds, the adults would customarily take word back to our parents regarding our misbehaviors. Such customary practices regularly resulted in severe parental punishment which was often coupled with the loss of childhood privileges.

As we grew older, my parents bought my brother and I our own bikes. These we rode everywhere, to the nearby stores, the playground and to explore new places. Most of our time, we spent swimming in mud holes, stealing peaches from our neighbor's trees, and shooting out the streetlights with our B.B. guns. Playing in and around the neighborhood, we felt quite safe. The other residents must have also felt quite safe for they all left their front doors unlocked even when they ran errands some distance away. It was a time when neighbors acted like one huge extended family.

After a few years in the Garden Oaks Community, we moved to Wildwood. Wildwood was the culmination of my mother and father's dream. At the time Wildwood epitomized the middle class suburb with tree-lined streets and well maintained lawns. Every adult member in the community went to work from nine to five; and, when at home, they seldom ventured outdoors. I didn't realize it at the time but Wildwood became my first contact with the up-and-coming in America. Everyone kept to themselves, seldom seeking friendly contacts with each other. To us, the children, this way of community life symbolized a very strange form of adult behavior. Gone was the reprimand children received from the elders. Gone was the trust of open doors. Gone was the throng of children bursting in and out of neighbors homes. In came the unfriendly stares of watchful neighbors; and in came the angry barks of dogs, replacing the laughter of children. I can't recall coming in contact with our neighbors at Wildwood. In fact, we were all estranged.

On the second day of our move to Wildwood, after a short outing, we arrived at home to find our picture window in the living room broken. This incident caused some alarm since we had moved into the community during the period when the white residents were gradually moving out. At the time we moved in, only a handful of white families remained. My father, aware of the racial divide, made no mention of the broken window to anyone for fear that it might stir pent-up racial hostilities. Instead of inquiring about the incident, he took no action choosing to remain low-keyed and let the incident die down as if it never happened. His inaction may have averted a potential strife.

CHAPTER 5
On Becoming An Alcoholic

Expelled from school, I rarely stayed in my community. I spent most of my time on the other side of town. There, I could walk the streets unrecognized. Why I chose this course of action, I am unsure. Maybe I felt too ashamed to let the people in my community learn of my academic failure, or that I had turned to a life of truancy and vagrancy.

Detached from my family, I also became increasingly detached from my community. My older brother, whom I adored, tried to talk to me about my behavior but I refused to listen. Slowly my parents' patience began to wear thin. First, they kept silent about my waywardness. Then they began to make comments about returning to school. When their hints did not bring about changes in my behavior, they resorted to remarks I considered minor threats. Each time they broached the subject of schooling to me, we ended up quarreling. The more they insisted, the more I resisted. It didn't dawn on me at the time that all they wanted was for me to return to school and acquire my high school diploma. From my standpoint, my parents had become my antagonists. They were always on my back for anything and everything. I couldn't do anything right for them. At least, this was what I thought.

To avoid my parents reproach, I tried to stay away from home as much as possible. I neither had a job nor was I attending school. My rebellious behavior made me afraid that my father would kick me out of the house if he knew that I was just hanging out with my friends all day. Yet, I did not change. Unbeknownst to me, my dad would come into my bedroom each night to check whether I had returned home. Each night he came, he found me passed-out in a state of drunkenness.

During the time I stayed away from home, I befriended a girl. A short time after our courtship, she became pregnant. Realizing my unprepared-ness to turn my life around, she left. After we parted company I realized how much I loved her but it was too late. Using our separation as an excuse, I began to drink excessively. In fact I stayed perpetually drunk.

One day, after repeated attempts to get me to reform failed, my dad said to me one day, "Junior, this house is too small for two big men to live in. You have wasted half of your life already and so you need to move on for good." Asking his son whom he named after him to leave his home for good must have pained my dad. How he felt, however, I would never know for he never spoke to me about it. He died while I was in prison.

My dad had kicked me out of the house before but not for long. Each time he did, I ended up on the other side of town drinking, sleeping in my friends' cars, and eating whatever I could find. It did not take very long for the police to take notice. Soon, several of them began to know me on sight. And soon thereafter, my public drunkenness kept me going in and out of jail. Imprisonment proved to be the loneliest times in my life. Yet, it did not serve as a deterrent to my alcoholism. Once in a while, I would find employment performing meaningless tasks, cleaning, mopping and running errands. No sooner I get paid, I would return to drinking nonstop and lose the job. The vicious cycle of getting hired and fired for drunkenness gripped my life with such force I couldn't muster the courage to seek out an exit. Instead, I wallowed in my drunken sorrow. The emotional pain dug deeply into my soul, and I refused to face the reality of an unsuccessful future. Unconsciously, I had chosen to live the life of a bum.

Awakened one morning after a prolonged period of drunkenness, I reasoned that I needed a change of environment to help break my habits as a dissolute young man. With this thought in mind, I decided to move to Wichita, Kansas to live with my father's sister. She welcomed me with open arms. I didn't waste any time trying to get my economic situation in order. Within a couple of weeks I landed my first job. The job came about as a result of talking to my aunt's male friend one evening as we watched television. He suggested that I apply for work at his workplace. I did so the very next day and was hired on the spot. The company, a commercial laundry business, supplied linens to hotels, restaurants, and an assortment of establishments. Acting on my aunt's friend recommendation, the supervisor gave me the job of emptying laundry bags. A few days after being hired I quit. It may be because of my laziness, but I rationalized it by saying that I wasn't ready to face the realities of a wage laborer.

Shortly after quitting, I obtained employment as a dishwasher at a restaurant. This job became the first enabler for my alcoholism. I worked the night shift and was usually in the dish room alone. Being alone provided me the opportunity to get beer from the walk-in cooler when no one was around. The pleasure of drinking on the job lasted about two weeks. I was fired because an inventory of beer in stock alerted management to the fact that I had been stealing and drinking every night.

Fired from the dishwashing job, I was hired as waiter at a golf and country club. This job enabled my drinking to become full blown. It was like a dream come true. The members of the club lived lives of luxury. Though a pauper, I felt like a prince among them. With bars located in every corner of the clubhouse, I took every opportunity to drink as much as I could. At nights, after work, I would drink until I could drink no more. My life, once again, became that of a perpetual drunk. I drank morning, noon and night. What a luxurious existence I thought.

As the weeks passed and I never sobered up, my aunt grew tired of my behavior.

"Junior," she said to me one day; "What has gotten into you child, you're constantly drunk; you need to do something with your life."

"Yes Mam," I replied, not wanting to hear her admonition.

"I don't know what your problem is, but you got to do something about it."

"I don't got no problem," I said after a short pause.

"If you ain't got no problem; How come you drinking so much?" my aunt snapped right back at me, then continued.

"How long you been like this Junior?"

I did not offer an answer. She turned as if to walk away from me then turned to face me again.

"Junior, you sure do have a problem, child. You need to get some treatment or something."

Not to be disrespectful to my aunt, I paused to hold my breath, then said.

"I don't need no treatment. I know what my problem is, and I can solve it myself."

"If you can solve it yourself, then, why don't you?" my aunt snapped as she walked out of the room.

The next day, I took the Greyhound bus back to Oklahoma. On the ride home, I kept thinking about what my aunt said that I have a problem. "I don't have a problem," I kept repeating to myself. "She doesn't know what she is talking about." Years later, as I entered drug and alcohol rehabilitation program, I came to the realization that my aunt was right. I did have a problem but chose denial as my form of defense.

Upon my return home to Oklahoma, my family welcomed me as if they had actually missed me, and during the first few days, treated me like royalty. I promised my parents that I would straighten up and get my life together. It felt good to be home again. Then, my homecoming fell into the routine of keeping in step with my brothers and sisters. During this period at home, I moved from one menial job to the next. For someone in search of financial security, these were not the type of jobs I aspired to keep until retirement.

Of the jobs I had, one in particular sticks out in my mind because it touched on my relationship with my father. After a succession of failures, the owner of a small restaurant hired me clean tables for the waitresses. Assigned the breakfast shift, I had to wake up early to be at the job on time. One morning, in the dead of winter, I was late for work so I awakened my father at five o'clock to give me a ride to the restaurant. Opening his eyes to look up at me he said, "Do you know what my father would have told me, if I woke him up at five o'clock in the morning to take me to work?" I did not answer the question for fear that he may not take me to work. He did, however, drive me to the restaurant without saying another word. I never asked him for a ride again.

For some time afterwards, I silently questioned my father's love for me. Then, an incident occurred that caused me to experience my father's affection first hand. One evening, while drinking with some of my associates, we got into and argument and one of them stabbed me with a knife. Two of the guys picked me up from the floor; put me in the car we traveled in, and rushed me home to my parents. Why they didn't take me to the hospital, I am not sure. When we arrived at my house, it seemed as if I had taken my last breath. One of the guys ran up to the door, and the next thing I remember was that my father took me out of the car, cradled me in his arms, placed me in the backseat of his car and rushed me to the hospital.

For a long time I could not understand how my father could show so much love for me, yet be so cruel by throwing me out on the streets to live like a bum, and letting me spend all of those lonely days and nights in jail. Now that I have a daughter, she may have questioned my integrity as a father in the same manner I questioned that of my father. Strange how age and experience play riddle with the soul.

CHAPTER 6
Highway To Homelessness

The sixties proved to be turbulent times for me. I was growing older and becoming more unstable. Unable to find employment, my father recommended me for a job at the motel where he worked. Each day, I would get to work late due to a hangover from the previous night's drinking. One day, my father cautioned me that if I went to work drunk, he would have my paycheck waiting for me. I didn't heed his warning. Once again, I went to work late due to a hangover. As soon as I arrived at work, my dad greeted with my check in his hand. Holding out the check to me, he asked, "Where are you going?" as if to let me know that I was no longer welcomed in his home. Unsure of myself, I asked half-heartedly:

"Can you take me to the bus station?"

"Where do you plan on going?" he queried with his head bent as if he was looking down for something.

"I think I'm going to go to California."

"California? That's interesting? What do you plan to do there?"

"I don't know. Maybe I can get a job, work for a while, then go some place else."

My dad did not say anything else. After waiting for me to cash the check, he drove me to the bus station without uttering a word. As he was about to let me out of the car he said, "Look up your uncle when you get to California, he may be able help some."

"Thanks dad," I said as I watched him drove away.

The bus ride to Los Angeles took three days. I had a lot of time to think, to reflect. I didn't know my exact destination, or what lay ahead of me. All I knew was that I had to move on. I thought of my brother and the good times we shared. He was now serving in the navy. I thought of my sisters and wondered whether they would miss me as I would, them. From their days as toddlers, I acted as one of their primary guardians. I could see their innocent faces as they called out to me, "Junior, come see this. Junior, can I go play? Junior, can I have a drink?" It was always, "Junior this, Junior that." Would I ever see them again? My life had taken many twists and turns, ups and downs, but I never imagined a sudden separation from my family. I also never imagined that the journey to California would be the beginning of my protracted struggle with homelessness.

I arrived in Los Angeles, California at the time the Vietnam War raged in full force. War protestors assembled in every street corner. Hippies and peace activists flocked every tavern, every park. Love could be felt everywhere. Having nowhere to go, I took up residence at the Greyhound bus station for a couple of days. During the day, I panhandled to get money for wine and food. At nights, I returned to the bus station where I slept in a stall in the men's restroom. Observing me roam through the bus station for a few days, a bootblack who shined shoes in the basement of the station befriended me. He told me that he had bus tickets to go anywhere in California, "I can give you a ticket to wherever you want to go if you promise to send me the money when you get it," he said. With his offer, it didn't take long for me to decide to get out of Los Angeles. After giving it some thought as to where next I would like to go, I decided on San Diego, California. My decision to travel to San Diego was based on the hope of seeing my older brother and some of the guys with whom I grew up, all of whom supposedly were stationed there.

Arriving in San Diego, I went to the Red Cross and asked for help in locating my brother and my friends. There, a gentleman told me that my brother's ship, the U.S.S. Kitty Hawk, an aircraft carrier, had left for the Ton Kin Bay in Vietnam. He also informed me that I would not be able to send my brother a message because of security concerns. I did, however, find out from the Red Cross that one of my friends was stationed at the Long Beach Naval station, in Long Beach, California. I was happy to have this information in case of need.

Night fell and I had no place to go. As time wore on, it became extremely cold. Left with little choice, I went to police station and asked where I could go to be out of the cold and get some sleep. Taking a quick look at my physical state, the policeman in charge decided to book me in the jail as a sleep-in. I must have slept quite well for I can't recall hearing anything or waking up during that night. The next day, released into the streets, I looked around at nothing in particular then made the decision that I must find a way to survive.

Broke and homeless in San Diego, I started begging for money to stay alive. Initially, I found begging painful. The rejections, and sometimes insults from people, pierced through the core of my Being. Like "Adam" in the Garden of Eden, I wanted to hide but where would I go? Having little choice, I continued to beg as a way to pull myself out of starvation. Within a few days, the pains of begging began to ware off, and shortly thereafter pride no longer deterred me from resorting to begging again. I had dirtied my Soul. I had nothing else left, no pride, no ethics, and no sense of morality. Within a very short period, I became a bona fide bum. Begging became my mode of survival, and gradually it emptied me of my own humaneness. Socially, I became a deviant who would use begging over and over again as a method of survival.

With begging came other consequences that brought me face to face with the San Diego police. On several occasions, the cops picked me up for vagrancy and threw me in jail for a day or two. Tired of such harassment, I decided to hitchhike out of town. Thumbing a ride out of town proved more difficult than I thought. The road leading to the freeway restricted certain types of travel, and carried signs which stated: **Two-Wheeled Vehicles Only** and **No Pedestrians**. In violation of the posted signs, I walked to the freeway. On my way, a police car passed by heading into town. My heart skipped a beat. I was leaving town because of the police and now I am going to be taken back into town by the police. What luck? As the car approached I saw someone in the back seat and I breathed a sigh of relief. They were not going to pick me up after all. I hurried through the rest of my way braving the heat from the blazing sun.

CHAPTER 7
My First Encounter With Angels

Vehicle after vehicle roared down the highway at varying speeds ignoring my raised thumb. Then, a car pulling a small trailer passed on by. Suddenly, it stopped ahead of me. I ran towards it, got in, and thanked the man again and again for picking me up.

"Where are you going?" he asked.

"Los Angeles" I replied.

"Live there?'

"No."

"Got any relatives there?"

"No. I'm going to see some friends there," I lied.

After this bit of conversation, we rode in silence for about twenty minutes. The man then pulled off the highway and let me know that he had reached his destination. He gave me a bag and told me to get some grapefruits out of the trailer. I thanked him again, got the grapefruit, and waved goodbye.

With the grapefruits and my scanty possessions in hand, I walked down the freeway losing all sense of time as the sun sank slowly in the horizon. Exhausted after a long walk, I finally came upon a little town where an elderly white couple offered me food and a night's rest. The next morning, after washing up, I went back to the room to get the rest of my things. There, I discovered that the couple had left me some money which they placed on top of my baggage. Their generosity moved me to tears. Somehow, I knew that the Lord was with me, and that I had a purpose in life. Like *Guardian Angels*, the elderly couple came into my path carrying out God's work. It seemed as if they were awaiting my arrival. I was a lost soul on long journey; I knew not what lay ahead of me, only what I had already suffered. To this day, the thoughtfulness of the elderly couple lingers in my mind. They gladly offered their home, their food and their money to a young black man who just walked in from the streets. They did not query or expressed reservations. They opened up their hearts and their home with such divine grace even a bum like me had to appreciate their noble deed.

Leaving the elderly couple's home, I caught a ride that took me to Oceanside, California, the home of the United States Marines. The atmosphere appeared tense throughout the town because of the Vietnam War. Bus loads of Marines rumbled through the streets carrying young men for shipment to the distant war. An eerie feeling seemed to have gripped the town. After two days I decided to move on. Concocting a story that I was a Marine ready to be shipped out to war, I begged enough money for a bus ticket to Los

Angeles. "I needed the money for an emergency visit home," I explained to passersby.

Before night fell, I joined the bus headed for Los Angeles. Arriving in Los Angeles, I decided to find a way to get to Long Beach. I had seen enough of Los Angeles. It depressed me. I still had a little money left from my Oceanside begging. It was not much, but at least I wasn't broke. From conversations with people, I learned that a city bus called the Freeway Flier would take me to Long Beach.

For some unknown reason, I went to Travelers Aid when I got to Long Beach. I didn't think anyone there would assist me but something within me said to try anyway. It felt as if I was being guided by an invisible hand. At the Aid office, the lady with whom I spoke was very pleasant. She made me feel as if I had come into contact with another *Guardian Angel*. She listened to my story then gave me a voucher that took care of my rent for ten days at the old Y.M.C.A. She also authorized an additional ten dollars a day for my meals. As required by policy, each day, I would return to the Aid office to pick up the money and a job referral.

The room given to me at the "Y" looked like something out of a Victor Hugo novel. It seemed perfect for a starving artist. My first night there I bought a cheap bottle of wine, and some cheese and crackers for dinner. I cried a lot in that room. Being homeless seemed to have wrenched from my young Soul, my sense of worthiness. Indeed, I am responsible for my circumstances. But how does a young high school drop-out who spent most of his youthful years in drunken stupor know the consequences of his indiscretions? I am not the product of a single parent. I did not have an unhappy childhood. What is it in me that led me toward this path of homelessness? As my mind beat up on my Soul in silent discourse, my flowing tears stung my parched face as a reminder of my frailty. Suddenly, I began to cry uncontrollably. The "Y" was only a temporary respite for my troubled Soul.

CHAPTER 8
Fighting To Survive In California

One day, the lady at the Aid center referred me to a Jack-In-The-Box fast food restaurant for employment. I got the job and held on to it for a couple of days. Living some distance away, and with no transportation, I lost the job for being habitually late. Meanwhile, I decided to get in touch with my friend stationed at the Long Beach Naval facilities.

Located on Ocean Avenue, the Long Beach Naval Station could easily be reached by bus. One day, I decided to go in search of my friend. At the gate of the station, I asked the sailor on duty if he knew the whereabouts of Earl Booker. He informed me that Earl was on the Harry S. Hubbard and that if I waited there, a bus would come by which I can take to the ship. Some minutes later the bus did arrive with other passengers. Joining it, we rode to a ship docked some distance away. The area looked huge. We arrived at what looked like a massive parking lot, but instead of cars, there were ships in berths plugged into the dock with giant electrical plugs. The dock had vending machines that dispensed hot Campbell's soup. I had never seen such things before. After waiting for about ten minutes, Earl Booker came staggering down the ramp leading to the dock.

"Hey Junior, what a surprise man," Earl said as he approached me with open arms. He gave me a big bear hug saying, "I am so happy to see you, what's up with you these days?"

"I came upon some hard times and decided to move West," I said.

"Any luck?" Earl asked.

"No man, I've been struggling."

"Come on Junior, you were always one to survive."

"Times have changed man, and things got really tough in Oklahoma so I had to leave."

"But why man, why? Why don't you join up and let the military help you straighten things out?"

"Come on Earl, you know me. Can't hold a job, been in and out of jail, been drinking and drugging for years now; what would the military do with someone like me?"

"Brother, what you telling me man, the military would take anybody willing to go Nam. They would take a jive-ass junkie if he can carry a gun." We both laughed at the last comment.

"How are things back home?" Earl asked?

"I don't know man, I haven't kept contact with anyone."

"So where are you bunking?"

"I am staying at the "Y" for a few days; after that I don't know."

After Earl Booker and I talked some more, I left to join the bus back to the Naval Station's entrance.

A few days after visiting Earl, things started going down hill in Long Beach. My time ran out at the "Y" with no improvement to my precarious circumstances. I went to live with my friend from Oklahoma City, one whom Earl Booker had taken me to see. Earl stayed there on and off while he was in port. Failing to adjust to my new situation I became restless. I wandered the streets aimlessly, drinking cheap liquor and sleeping in any hole I could find. A few days later, I was arrested for public drunkenness and served ten days at the Long Beach pea farm. Tired of being in and out of jail and harassed by the police, I decided to do something about it.

Following up on my conversation with Earl, I went to the Marine recruiter and tried to enlist. I told him about my criminal record, but he guaranteed me that enlistment would not be a problem. He signed me up then bused me and other potential recruits to Los Angeles for a physical exam. I knew that I had a bad eye due to an injury I suffered a few years earlier, but I was not going to let this deter me from passing the exam. Traveling on the bus, I tried to convince myself that I had to pass the exam. Upon our entry into the exam room, I took off my clothes, placed them in the little basket that they gave to everyone, and then anxiously followed the yellow line to the examiner. The initial scrutiny rolled along smoothly until time came to take the eye test. The examiners tried everything to allow me to pass the test, but I failed. "Try the army," they said at the conclusion of their examination, "They might take you."

Overcome by disappointment, I decided not to return to Long Beach. I had no reason for going back so I bummed around downtown Los Angeles for a few days. One day, I happened upon an employment agency that was recruiting people to pick oranges. I signed up. "What do I have to lose?" I thought to myself.

The orange groves turned out to be the worst place I had ever seen in my life. Several filthy dorms stood in a corner of the groves. The dorm assigned to me was no better than the rest. It seemed to house a lot more than people; rotted foods, flies, maggots and a variety of bugs. Around the dorms, Mexican immigrants gathered almost everywhere. Their foods - rice, refried beans, and tacos - were staples and served at every meal. The Mexicans loved it; I hated it. About a half mile down the road from the grove stood a little store that gave credit to the workers. The fastest selling products were wine and cigarettes. I stayed drunk on these bestsellers. It was my way of coping with the unbearable conditions.

Each day at the orange groves, I wondered how the Mexican immigrants coped. They spent strenuous hours in the field picking tons and tons of oranges. They worked with such precision they made me feel ashamed. They never complained, at least not openly. Working in silence, they carried loads of oranges that seemed much heavier than their body weights. In the evenings, they would sit outside their dorms in groups chatting and laughing as if they had had a joyous time in the groves. As for me, each day brought me greater aches and pains. Sometimes my entire body ached. To deal with my misery, I consumed large quantities of alcohol which made me pass out in drunkenness.

As soon as I received my first pay check from working in the orange groves, I left and went back to Los Angeles. Running out of options, I felt I would be better off dead. Nothing worked for me. Once again, I stumbled my way around downtown Los Angeles. One day, I went into a car wash on Ventura Boulevard and quite unexpectedly got a job. The guy with whom I worked was an ex-convict from Oklahoma. Instantly, we became friends and started hanging out together. Two ex-cons from Oklahoma in a Los Angeles car wash, what are the odds? The guy had a 1957 Chrysler with a bad master brake cylinder. The car's defect did not deter us from riding around town in "style". We constantly poured brake fluid in it so the brakes wouldn't collapse. Besides being our means of transportation, the car also served as our home. We drove it during the day, and slept in it at nights. I am sure we were not the only people driving around in their so called "home."

One day my friend and I decided to go to San Francisco. After receiving our paychecks that evening, we headed out. Without much thought, we took the old west coast highway 101 that went around the mountains. We were lucky to make it in the car, given the condition of the brakes.

It was December 1965. We pulled into San Francisco. Coming down a hill on one the streets, the car brakes failed. After swiping a few parked cars and street signs, the car came to a complete stop upon hitting a wall. I am not sure if we were dazed from the wreck or from our drugging and drinking; nevertheless, we got out alive and started bumming around San Francisco. The joyousness of Christmas permeated everywhere. San Francisco is truly the most beautiful city that I have ever visited. The boats in the harbor decked with their Christmas lights sparkled in the night's darkness. Along the fisherman's wharf, the smell of a variety of cooked fish filled the air as a signal of *welcome to the city of love*. As days went by, I walked throughout the Filmore district dreaming about being wealthy. On one occasion, I went up to the park on Knob Hill, Haight Asbury. It was where the hippies usually gathered. I didn't see anyone. I felt disappointed.

For a few days, my friend and I took up residence at a cheap hotel, amidst the trash previous customers left behind. It was all we could afford. Each day my friend left the hotel early, only to return at nights with handfuls of dollar bills. These he joyfully spread out on the bed telling me to take a few bucks. Where, and how he got the money, I am not sure. I could only surmise that the guy was a good thief. Afraid to be caught with him, I left.

Inquiring into job possibilities, several stragglers told me that I could find work at the longshoreman's hall close to the embarcadero. To my dismay, the hall turned out to be simply a hang-out for longshoremen. Not knowing what to do, I just walked away in confusion.

❧

CHAPTER 9
Arrested And Sent Back To Oklahoma

With my friend no longer with me, I bummed around San Francisco for a couple of days. Drinking heavily and roaming the streets, the police arrested me and threw me in jail for being a public nuisance. Upon gaining my release from jail, I decided to return to Los Angeles. Apparently, I couldn't run from my fate; I was destined to live the life of a bum in Los Angeles.

I arrived in Los Angeles and nothing had changed. Everywhere I turned, I encountered dead ends. I then started hanging out on Fifth and Los Angeles Street helping other bums begging money for wine. Thus, I stayed drunk and down and out. Ill luck soon followed. One day two plain-clothes policemen arrested me for begging and took me to the Los Angeles county jail. At my court appearance, the female judge asked me for information regarding my mother and father. She promised to get in contact with them. If they send me a money order and a bus ticket to get home, she would let me go. Knowing that my parents had given up on me, I went back to the cell fully convinced that I would be sent to the California reformatory. The possibility of serving jail time in California made me feel alone in the world. Why did she have to contact my parents? Why didn't she just release me with a warning? When I went back to court the judge gave me a bus ticket along with a money order my parents had sent for me to get home. She ordered my release and wished me well. The manner in which the judge treated me touched me with the warmth and mercy of a *Guardian Angel*. Her decision to sentence me home instead of prison must have saved my life. I was on a downward spiral, speedily drinking myself into oblivion. The judge seemed to have sensed my decline and gave me a chance to redeem myself, and even though I did not succeed in doing so, her decision did give me time for pause.

※ ※ ※

Today, not too many individuals are given such a chance. The emphasis on punishment, three strike laws, overzealous prosecutors, judges unwilling or unable to empathize, all contribute to more youngsters being placed in correctional facilities, and for longer periods. In volunteering with the Florida A & M University, Role Model Program, I sometimes became saddened by children's stories of arrests and the judicial sentences imposed on them. Many of these kids were not old enough to be teenagers. Were their judges as empathetic as the one who sentenced me to my parents' home? From my conversations with several of the kids, sentences like the one I received are rare, especially for at-risk youths.

᙮ ᙮ ᙮

Cashing the money order from Oklahoma that the judge handed me proved difficult at first. I tried several places and failed. Finally, a convenience store owner accepted it for a fee. Giving in to temptations, I rented a cheap room, bought a bottle of wine and got drunk. This caused me to return to Oklahoma a day later than the judge ordered.

I arrived in Oklahoma in the dead of winter. Having no coat, I walked home from the bus station with just the clothes I had on. The bitingly cold wind pierced my skin, and left me numb by the time I reached my parents house.

As soon as I knocked on the door, my mother opened it and hugged me. She slept on the sofa, she said, because she knew I would be home that day. She told me to go and let my father know that I was home. I went into my parents' bedroom and said, "Daddy I'm home." My dad took one look at me and noticing my Afro hairstyle said, "Look on the dressing table and get you enough money to get a haircut." Given all my struggles, my dad's remarks sounded surprisingly cold. I guess, I expected him to say something like, "I am glad you are home son," or, "Welcome home Junior." I found it difficult to read his feelings or reactions. I consoled myself by reasoning that if he didn't care he wouldn't have sent me the money for my passage home. But, what if he really didn't care? Would he turn me out again? These questions lingered in my mind for a while, and left me with conflicted feelings about parental affection.

CHAPTER 10
Wrongful Arrest And Imprisonment

Back home in Oklahoma, it didn't take long to resurrect my old habits of drinking and hanging out with other bums. Clearly, I couldn't, or didn't want to stop drinking. As before, each day I would leave home, drink as much as I could until late into the night; I would then stagger my way back home. Several times the cops arrested me for public drunkenness, getting into fights or being a public nuisance. As my addiction to alcohol and drugs increased, my arrest rates also increased.

One day, after several hours of drinking and smoking reefer with an acquaintance, we decided to go to a friend's apartment. Upon arrival at the housing complex where the friend resided, I felt dazed and decided to wait in my acquaintance's car. Drifting in and out of my dizziness, I thought hours had passed, and that my acquaintance would not be back. Upon regaining some semblance of consciousness, I drove the car back to the club leaving my friend behind. Realizing that I had driven off with his car, my acquaintance reported it stolen. It didn't take long for the cops to show up at the club and arrest me. With the car back in my acquaintance's possession, I thought that I would be released. Instead, the police detained me for pre-trial hearing because I couldn't post bond. At the hearing, my acquaintance showed up and testified against me. Knowing that I did drive off with the car, I plea-bargained and agreed to serve three years probation.

Back on bad terms with my family, I once again drifted from relative to relative. At the same time, my ex-girlfriend regularly harassed me about not supporting her child who claimed was my daughter. Occasionally, I found work but did not earn enough to support myself, much less anyone else. Financially, I barely existed.

One night in 1967, my roving lifestyle came to an abrupt end. At odds with most of my relatives because of my intolerable behavior, I decided to spend the night with my brother and his family. After watching the ten o'clock news with my sister-in-law and the children, we went to bed. I slept on the floor, which, for me, was a step up from sleeping on the street or in an abandoned car. Worn out from days of drinking, I didn't hear my brother come in that night from work. Early in the morning, however, I heard a knock on the door. Unaware of what was in store for me, I got up and opened the door. "Is your name Ulyses Hooks?" the voiced rang out before I could clear my sleepy eyes. It was the police. "We would like for you to come with us to headquarters downtown for questioning," the cop said. When my brother intervened, they informed him that they would take me back home when they finished their questioning.

Knowing that I had not done anything wrong, I stepped out onto the porch. Immediately, the cops grabbed me roughly by the arms, handcuffed me, and literally threw me into the back seat of the police car. For three days they held me in the city jail. They then transported me to the Oklahoma county jail on a charge of second-degree burglary. I stood accused of burglarizing the "Freedom Center", a black community empowerment organization. The burglar, they alleged, stole a typewriter. Supposedly, they had an eyewitness who placed me on the scene. I stood before them in shock because I didn't commit the crime. Furthermore, at the time of the robbery, I was at my brother's house watching the ten o'clock news with my sister-in-law and the children. They all were my alibis.

Days went by and I was still in jail for a crime I didn't commit. At first, I thought they would find the real burglar and then release me. If this didn't happen, I felt I would be tried and acquitted. Then, the days turned into weeks. I was still in jail without a trial. Gradually, my hopes turned into fear. What if a jury does not believe me and finds me guilty? I toyed with this question over and over causing my mind to play tricks on me. Some times I was quite confident, and other times, I became intensely afraid. Each time family members visited, I asked their help in finding the identity of the real burglar. During the day, I kept mostly to myself, praying and hoping for a positive outcome to my plight. During the night I would lay awake for hours pondering the question, "Why me, why me Lord?" My wavering thoughts drove me to the brink of insanity but somehow I managed to pull back.

Making some inquires on his own, my younger brother Craig found out who had committed the crime. He tried to get the person to confess, but the guy refused. To prove my innocence, I wrote a letter to the director of the organization telling her that I did not commit the burglary and to please investigate. I never heard from her. Left with no other recourse, I waited for the justice system to do its work in protecting the innocent person. Six months after my arrest, and still in jail, the court authorities scheduled my trial.

❧ ❧ ❧

Incarceration forced me to think more about the practices of the judicial system. Prior to my arrest, I grew up believing that the justice system was fair. I also believed that everyone arrested is entitled to a speedy trial. I became confused. The police arrested me for a crime I didn't commit, and months passed before the court scheduled my trial. What is wrong with the system? Some may think that I am like any other criminal, denying that I committed the crime. The truth is, I neither stole the typewriter nor broke into the Freedom Center. Yes, I was in and out of jail, each time for minor offenses, drunk and disorderly, fist fights etc., but never for any serious crimes. I can hear the unconvinced shouting, "Yeah, that's what they all say when they get caught. Innocent! My foot." I too would have said the same had I not experienced the injustice of the justice system, first hand.

❧ ❧ ❧

Trial day arrived giving my spirit a boost. Almost immediately, the prosecutor verbally pounced upon me making me seem lower than the lowest animal. I felt dazed and dehumanized. Yes, me, a habitual drunk feeling dehumanized. Listening to the prosecutor's diatribe, I began to lose interest in the case. A puny man with a big mouth I thought. A few minutes into the trial, I could no longer hear nor see anything. I couldn't even tell if the so called jury of my peers was all white.

My court appointed attorney did not allow me to testify at the trial because of my prior arrests. My sister-in-law, however, testified. She truthfully informed the court that she, her children and I were at her house watching the news at the time of the robbery. In rebutting her testimony, the prosecutor told the jury that anyone would lie to save a relative from being convicted. He then called to the witness stand, a black male whom I did not know nor had seen before. The man lied that he saw me standing in the door-way of the "Freedom Center" with a typewriter. He said he was positive because his car headlights shone on me. After a feeble defense by my attorney, the jury went into deliberation. Shortly thereafter, they came back with a guilty verdict. It is difficult to describe how I felt, for though my mother and baby brother sat in the courtroom as my sources of comfort, I lost awareness and no longer saw their faces.

Watching her son adjudicated guilty for a crime he didn't commit must have pained my mother. Like the many mothers before her, she must have stared at my back as the guards led me out of the courtroom in chains. She must have cried for the son she brought forth into this world, the one who seemed to have lost his sense of reality, the one who tried to hide from the vicissitudes of life through the routine of daily drunkenness. It must have pained her to know that she tried to help her son the best way she could, but failed in her efforts. In the quiet comforts of her home, she must have cried. Being led out of the courtroom, all of these things ran through my mind. Were they real or imagined? I do not know. With my back towards my family, I could not see their expressions.

In 1968, I arrived at the Oklahoma State Penitentiary after being slapped with a ten year sentence for second degree burglary, and three years for probation violation. The judge ruled that the sentences must be served consecutively. Continuing to profess my innocence, prison officials immediately labeled me a nut case and placed me in receiving cell thirteen. I prayed to God nearly everyday in that cell. Before, I used to wonder why people called on God only in times of crisis. Being in a jail cell changed my perception.

Throughout my ordeal, I felt my faith was being tested, and that it would soon be over. In my view, the fabricated arrest, the kangaroo trial and false imprisonment existed only in books. It didn't happen to innocent people like me. It took a while for reality to set in, and when it did, I lost faith in everything. God, justice, and the love of mankind manifested themselves as a bunch of baloney. Men in power could do to the poor almost anything they wanted. And, if you happen to be a minority, God forbid; you lack the influence or power to set things right. I know I was innocent. Insisting on this fact proved to be detrimental.

The prison authorities kept me at the Oklahoma State penitentiary for several weeks of psychological and psychiatric evaluations. I guess they were looking for a way to destroy me completely. To label someone as crazy is like signing his death warrant. The evaluations ended the same way they started, i.e., abruptly. Apparently, my age at the time of arrest surfaced as a major issue. As a result, prison officials decided to transfer me to the Oklahoma State Reformatory in Granite, Oklahoma. At the time, the Oklahoma State Reformatory served as a quasi-prison for first time young offenders.

In the reformatory, it didn't take long for me to adjust to a life behind bars. I had grown up with just about everyone there who came from Oklahoma City. The unwritten rule purported that if you form alliances with your homeboys you would survive. I did just that. Looking back, I am convinced that the inmates in the reformatory were not considered as true human beings but as society's rejects. I, for sure, was one of them. I had a warm bed, three hot meals, and no meaningful responsibility or rehabilitation treatment. Under these circumstances, my life as a convict gradually took shape, and I began to adjust to prison norms. Within a short while behind bars, my discomforts decreased and my comfort level began to increase. Concomitantly, my attitudes and behavior also changed causing concerns among state reform officials. Keeping track of my activities, they accused me of being the leader of a gang that regularly violated institutional rules, and influenced others to be disruptive. Their accusations led to my transfer back to the Oklahoma State Penitentiary (Big Mack). After the transfer, I realized that the reformatory had trained me to accommodate to prison lifestyle.

It is almost impossible for me to describe the complexities of the prison system given my subjective perceptions as an inmate. From what I observed, Oklahoma State Penitentiary was not unique. Like the many other State Penitentiaries in the nation, it operated like a self-supporting micro-city within a larger city. In some respects it operated somewhat like a manufacturing industry producing furniture, clothes, mattresses, brooms, canned goods, and meat products. Inmates supplied the labor power. Favorite inmates and their prison guard friends served as supervisors and managers respectively. Manufacturing followed the assembly line methods with finished products packaged and shipped to warehouses for sale in various market sectors.

Most of my time in the Oklahoma State penitentiary I spent fighting my case through the post-conviction appeals process. My efforts proved futile; for each time I tried, I failed to get my case overturned. After serving three and a half miserable years behind bars, I accepted a parole. Initially, I thought the parole board would reject my request. One elderly gentleman bombarded me with questions regarding my prospective readjustment to mainstream society in so many different ways that his questioning began to play games with my patience. I became irritable and tried desperately to control my anger. Realizing that he would not relent in his line of questioning until he received a plausible answer, I made up a story of how I found enlightenment while incarcerated and planned to lead a righteous life after my release. Looking straight at me, his lips twisted slightly into a faint smile. I knew there and then that my chances for parole were quite good.

Why I claimed a religious awakening, I am not sure. Perhaps the Lord did touch my Soul, but in my bitterness with the world, I failed to recognize the Divine guidance. It would take years of self inflicted misery and a host of helping hands to make me grasp the extent of this Spiritual connection.

CHAPTER 11
Released From Prison And Feelings of Alienation

In my introductory sociology class in college, my professor talked excitedly about culture and society, and the roles we all play in our everyday lives. Conformity to norms, adaptation to different situations, all these things sound good in the classroom but what applications do they have in real life situations? Many of the things he talked about sounded like life in a prison. As a matter of fact, my life in mainstream society was that of a bum. In prison, I had several friends and we conformed to our own group norms, albeit prison norms. New prisoners who demonstrated a willingness to adapt found themselves accepted into their chosen groups. And together, the network of groups operated as a quasi-community with its own customs and culture. Failure to abide by group norms resulted in various types of sanctions, including ostracism.

Each class period, as my professor ranted and raved about life in society, I couldn't help recalling my life behind bars. The things he talked about seemed more real to me when I lived in prison and not outside of it. To me, the comradery, the solidarity, codes of everyday conduct, social status and respectability, seemed as if my professor was describing the social relations within prison walls. Perhaps it was this perception of prison relations that contributed to my failure as a parolee.

❦ ❦ ❦

Released from prison on parole, my sister made the long trip from Oklahoma City to McAlester, Oklahoma to pick me up. On the journey home with my sister, I had some time to think between conversations. I had no plans for life away from prison, and my qualifications were zero. Within me raged a fierce battle that started with my arrest and imprisonment for a crime I did not commit. Being in prison, and listening to convicts brag about their crimes, initially made me feel like a traitor. I had little to contribute to prisoners' conversations. I tried to act cool, and pretended to be a bona fide member of their rebellious social world. Strange, how a person adapts to his new circumstances through association and regular interaction! At first, I kept to myself but then the need for belongingness crept up upon me. Gradually, I sought acceptance in the prison groups. Integration into the elite group, however, depended on one's criminal history, and mine was considered feeble. In the world of convicts, the severity of the crimes committed symbolized honorability. Isn't it amazing that in the arena of "dishonorables", the most "dishonorabled" was regarded as the most honorable?

The crime I supposedly committed fell into the category of lesser honor, but it did gain me membership into the "*fraternal order of convicts*".

Being out on parole, my soul soon began to ache. I had no sense of community, no sense of belonging. Old habits die hard and soon I returned to a life of drinking and getting into fights. Silently, I reasoned that if ever I was to return to prison, it would be for a crime I did commit, one that I could boast about, one that would indicate how successful I would be in the future. As an inmate, I had friends I could count on. They needed me and I needed them. And, whenever I listened to my prison buddies brag about their indiscretions, I wanted to be like them. But, how could I? I did not commit the crime which landed me in jail. Moreover, prisoners didn't consider stealing to be a crime of "high status", and stealing a typewriter was pretty low on their totem pole.

Weeks after my parole, life behind bars rested heavily on my mind. Confused and disoriented, I found it difficult to cope with release especially since I lacked the support necessary to reform my life and be a productive citizen. Unable to find a steady job after several weeks, I became increasingly alienated from my family and friends. The more detached I became from my loved ones, the more I missed hanging out with my prison buddies. I missed their comradery, their boasts, their taunting and grinning. From some of the fellows who gained their releases after me, I learned of the changes that had taken place in prison. The more elaborate their stories became, the greater the urge in me to get arrested and sent back to prison. But, I also hated the darker side of prison life and swore not to return. Haunted by this inner turmoil, I began to drink heavily not knowing what direction to take. Thus, I became imprisoned in two different worlds with two separate realities. Outside of prison, I was invisibly trapped in the stigmatization of being an ex-con. Inside prison, I was visibly trapped in the narrow confines of reinforced concrete walls.

CHAPTER 12
Going Back To Prison

My cousin was the first person to visit me after I returned home from prison. At the time, he lived in the same apartment complex as my mother. One evening, I went to his apartment to say hello to his wife. Together they led me into their bedroom. There, displayed across the bed was an assortment of men's clothing, all slick and beautiful, all new.

"Pick out a wardrobe for yourself Junior," my cousin said to me.

"Nah man, I can't do that," I said reluctantly.

"Oh! Come on man, take the damn things."

"Are all these yours?" I asked sheepishly.

"If they were not mine what they'd be doing in my house?"

I picked up a pair of pants and stroked the smooth cloth with the palm of my hand.

"These feel real good," I muttered.

"Go ahead, they are yours," my cousin coaxed.

"What's the matter Junior, are you afraid?" my cousin's wife asked.

"Afraid? Afraid of what? I am not afraid." We all laughed.

"If you are not afraid, then why don't you take the damn things?"

I lifted the pants to my nose to smell the fabric, "This smells good," I said.

"Here try this, and this," the wife of my cousin said as she threw several pieces of clothes into my hands.

"Prison sho seem to change you Junior, you not been like this brother," my cousin said.

For a man just released from prison, my cousin's offer seemed like a journey into paradise. I also saw it as a path leading back to prison, something I did not want. But, it was also a way to craft my own crime, and elevate my status if I happened to be behind bars again. These conflicting feelings tormented me and I became engulfed in a daily emotional storm.

Each day I hung out with my cousin, I seemed to care less about being out on parole. Together we checked out the clubs, partied with ladies of the night in their motel rooms, and kept an eye out for a job. By job, I mean burglary. My cousin prided himself in breaking into businesses at nights. I rode with him as the "lookout." Burglary proved quite profitable and the money rolled in fast. For kicks, I started shooting (mainlining) heroin using the money from burglary to help maintain my habit. Heroin happened to be the in-thing at the time. Almost all of the guys with whom I grew up either used heroin or sold it. Life seemed easy. We stole, we shot heroin; we paid for it with money earned from selling stolen articles. The more we stole the greater amount of heroin we abused. The more heroin we abused, the more money we needed to support our habits, so the more we stole. With each cycle of stealing and abusing drugs came increasing desperation and an ever growing detachment from reality.

One night, we broke into a gas station, stole some tires and headed off to our "fence." On our way going, we happened to pass by another thief whom my cousin knew. We stopped to greet him. Seeing the tires in our car, the thief requested, in codes thieves understood, if he could be counted in. Declining his request, my cousin and I drove off. We must have traveled a distance of about five miles when suddenly, like birds of prey, police cars closed in from behind us. Realizing that the thief may have snitched on us for not including him, my cousin started speeding. The police followed in hot pursuit. I can't remember how fast we were traveling but I recall saying, "This time I am going to jail for something I did." After miles of high speed chase, we stopped at a friends' house and ran in. No sooner we entered the house; several police cars pulled up and surrounded it. Guns drawn, the cops shouted for us to "come outside" with our "hands up." Sensing that the situation could escalate, the lady who owned the house walked out to the police and told them that she would send us out. Stepping outdoors, the cops cuffed my cousin and I, and pushed us into separate squad cars for questioning. Knowing that he would likely be imprisoned for stealing, my cousin disavowed his role in the burglary and blamed everything on me. The cops then booked and released me on charges of concealing stolen property.

It is strange how a person's mind works. Mine was in overdrive. Before my arrest, I wanted to go back to prison for a crime I did commit. Given time to think between arrest and trial, however, I became unsure. I had violated my parole, and with my trial for burglary looming, I felt bitter and afraid; bitter because my cousin snitched, and afraid because of frightening newspaper accounts regarding the conditions in the Oklahoma State Prison. Headline after headline indicated that prison conditions could erupt into a riot at any time. With each report, my fears heightened as the likelihood of being imprisoned during the period of prison turbulence increased. Afraid of being caught in the midst of a prison riot, I asked my dad for assistance in securing a lawyer. He acquiesced, and we contacted an attorney who agreed to represent me. On our way to the attorney's office, I asked my dad if he could split the attorney's retention fees to cover part of my bond. He stopped, took a hard look at me with fury in his eyes and said, "That's the problem with black people, splitting things up and splitting it up until they don't have enough to cover a single problem." With that said, he remained silent the rest of the way to the attorney's office.

I am not sure how much money my dad gave the attorney but that soon ran out, and another attorney showed up to represent me at the hearing. This attorney, whom anyone could see as most incompetent, had already made a deal with the prosecutors. He accepted on my behalf, a plea of ten years imprisonment to be served consecutively for probation violation and concealing stolen property. When

I protested, the incompetent attorney angrily argued with me. He screamed that had he not made the deal, I would have had to spend a longer time in prison because of my past arrests, and my cousin's testimony against me. He ended by saying, "I've already made the deal and that's it." I guessed this meant that I should shut up and do my time.

⅔ ⅔ ⅔

I would relive my experience with poor legal representation many times more as I pursued my Masters Degree in Criminology, and working with at-risk youths in the communities around my university. Attending several juvenile and adult court hearings over the years, I have watched and listened to attorneys, pro-bono and public defenders alike, one after the other, announce the plea bargains of their poverty stricken clients, most of who happened to be black. "Your honor we accept … of six months in prison and a fine of …. Your honor my client has consented to the prosecutors offer of three years imprisonment with time served taken into consideration as part of the sentencing …."

In post-sentencing conversations with parents and relatives of the convicted, they all gave the same familiar explanations. "He/she was in jail before, and the lawyer says it doesn't look good …. To spend less time in jail we must accept a plea bargain." These comments were often accompanied by tears which in turn moved me to tears as they made me recall my own past. One incident that stood out in my mind happened the day I walked all the way out of the Leon County Courthouse with my eyes brimming with tears. I had accompanied my professor to court that day to listen to the trial of a student. Also on trial that day was a young father whose wife, mother and children were in attendance at his hearing. When the time came for his sentencing, the judge noted his prior arrests, announced his probation violation, along with his new charges, and imposed a sentence of thirty years.

Upon hearing the sentence, the mother, wife and children all began to cry. Jumping up quickly from his seat, an officer of the court rushed over and ushered the crying family members out of the courtroom. Just then, almost in slow motion, the young man twisted sideways from the officers holding on to him. As he turned his head to take a last glance of his loved ones exiting the room, one could see the sadness in the young man's face. "Could it be that the severity of his sentencing resulted from poor legal representation?" I asked myself as I walked away from the courtroom that day. I did not hear any legal arguments on his behalf. All I remembered was the judge asking, "Do you understand your plea?" Then, I saw the young man shaking his head up and down while answering, "Yes Mam." Did he truly understand the judge's question? I still wonder.

❧ ❧ ❧

Sentenced to ten years for probation violation and concealing stolen property, I decided that my imprisonment this time around must be different. I had actually committed the crime for which I was found guilty. Once again, I entered the Oklahoma State Penitentiary. Walking to the "chow hall" to eat, I would hear the guys who knew me from before saying, "I told you, he would be back." In some strange way, their comments served as a form of acceptance that somehow erased the mental anguish I suffered in going to prison the first time. My stay at the Oklahoma State Penitentiary, however, lasted for only a few days. Prison officials subjected me to various types of evaluations, and determined that I was addicted to drugs and alcohol. They then transferred me to Lexington Community Treatment Center for drug rehabilitation services.

Lexington, a medium security institution, housed prisoners convicted of alcohol and drug related crimes. Once there, convicts had to undergo a treatment regimen that would reduce their drug dependency, thereby enabling them to return to prison to serve out their sentences. Instead of a substance abuse treatment center, Lexington operated more like a drug promotion center. At every turn, and in every corner, one could see convicts smoking weed while holding conversations with each other. So severe was the proliferation of drugs at the institution, more than ninety percent of the convicts were said to be abusing drugs on a daily basis. As for me, Lexington became my drug haven. Morning, noon, and night, I sat around with other convicts smoking joint after joint of marijuana. Talking about the pleasures of exile, we lived it at the Lexington Center.

Like most substance abuse treatment centers, Lexington also had a positive side. The institution offered convicts the opportunity to earn their high school equivalency diploma. Aware of this opportunity, I took time for what I call creative educational explorations, and preparing for the G.E.D. I studied for a few hours, smoked some weed, then went back to my studies. My daily routine soon turned into a cycle of reading, smoking, reading, and smoking. A few months after I began studying, I wrote and passed the G.E.D. I then asked for and received permission to take the

A.C.T. exam at the University of Oklahoma. I took it and passed. Shortly thereafter, I was sent back to the Oklahoma State Penitentiary. The move made me realize that prison would sometimes aid you in becoming whole again and put you on the road to success before it crushes the Spirit it has helped to ignite in you.

CHAPTER 13
The Prison Riot

Back in prison, the warden assigned to me the task of runner. The responsibilities of runner came with a security clearance, enabling me to move freely about the institution as much as I pleased. With this new found freedom, I took every opportunity to make new acquaintances and formalize old relationships. Through my daily routines of moving about from one place to the other, I quickly learned about the discontent among prisoners. Plotting quietly through direct conversations, and at times through silent language, prisoners honed their plan for revolt. I am not sure how the plotters selected or influenced their accomplices to join them. Once, however, I overheard a short conversation between two black convicts. On their way to their cells one said to the other:

"Hey bro, you gonna join in the hunga strike?"

"Nah bro, I ain't gonna?" the second responded.

"Why? You afraid?" asked the first.

"No. Shit no. Afraid? Who's afraid?" replied the second, sounding somewhat agitated.

"Then, why not join in?"

"Join who? Dem white boys? The hunga strike is for dem white boys who already got their food stashed in their cells. Dey na gonna starve?"

"Who told you that?"

"Nobody. Any fool could see how they done bought up the commissary."

A few days later, it became clear that the hunger strike was a prelude to the disturbances and riot that followed.

Early one morning, in between shifts, and at a time that seemed less likely, prisoners, led by a muscular blond fellow grabbed the captain of the guards, hit him on the head and fell him to the floor. At that moment, I was on my way through the rotunda running errands. Suddenly the director of the Classification Office signaled me to hurry up and get out of sight. He had observed the brewing turmoil from his position upstairs. And, realizing my unawareness of the unfolding events, he frantically tried to get my attention so that I could be out of harms way. Without a second delay, I ran, and barely made it through the gate which banged loudly as it closed behind me. Running up the metal stairs leading to the Classification Office, I took a momentary glance backwards and could see the rotunda as it erupted in chaos. Prisoners were running every which way. Immediately upon reaching the top stair, the director whisked me into the Classification Office just before the door slammed shut behind me.

Upon my entry, I found the Classification Office already filled with other inmates, many of whom worked there. For some time, we sat speculating as to what was happening. I don't recall how long we spent wondering about the situation, but it seemed like a long time. Suddenly, the phone rang, hushing us into silence. The caller, who happened to be from one of the prison industrial production units, told the Classification Office clerk that they were going to burn the prison down. As soon as the clerk hung up the phone, it rang again. It was a prisoner from another production unit calling to say they were going to burn their unit down. After his call, another came, then another, until all of the prison industrial production units made similar reports of intended destruction.

At the time of the riot, the McAlister prison was racially segregated. It had two recreation yards, one for black and the other for white prisoners. Overlooking the white recreation yard was the Classification Office in which we sought refuge. Form there we could see clearly the events unfolding below. White convicts had plundered the canteen, and stacked the foodstuffs they stole in their designated recreation yard. Not knowing how long the turmoil would last, the white prisoners in the Classification Office began letting down strings. On these, the prisoners in the recreation yard tied various food items for us to eat. In the process of securing food, a commotion ensued. A rebel convict grabbed the deputy warden around his neck while another held a knife to his head. Almost instantly, the white prisoner who ran the Classification Office screamed, "Don't kill him or you will never get out alive." Hearing his admonition, the rebel prisoners left the yard dragging the warden along. We then withdrew from the Classification Office windows as the mob of prisoners ran about in wild fury.

Some time after we retreated from our positions near the windows, prison guards came in and began hauling prisoners out in groups of ten. Soon after each group was taken, bursts of gunfire followed. Personally, I was scared. I thought that the guards were shooting the prisoners they had carried out of the office. I then maneuvered my way to be among the last group of prisoners to be taken. When the prison guards came, they marched us to a waiting bus for transportation to McAlister city jail.

After the riot, prison officials shipped all the convicts to various medium security camps. For a while we lost sense of our location, or where next we would be shipped. Trucked from place to place prevented prolonged contacts among the convicts. It appeared prison officials intentionally did things this way in an effort to gather information on the key planners of the riot. Keeping convicts on the move, out of prolonged contact with one other, made it almost impossible for them to share information and establish corroboration. It took several moves and over several months, for us to finally move back into Oklahoma State Penitentiary. Upon returning there, I was dumb struck at what I saw; the charred remain of the prison looked like one huge barbecue pit.

The initial move back to Oklahoma State Penitentiary caused some anxieties, but within a week, I began to adjust to the daily routines of prison life. I can't recall anyone discussing the riot, but one could see that the incident had taken a toll on the prison administration and on the convict population as well. The uneasiness between prisoners and guards lasted for some time as each group looked upon the other with some degree of suspicion. Even among the convicts the chit chat and idle talks seemed to have ceased. Prior to the riot, conversations went something like this:

"Hey Leroy, did you see they brung Slick back in last night?"

"Nah man. What he do this time, steal a pig or something?"

"No. Ah hear he stole some damn ole TV from the pawn shop."

"I tole you the brother ain't got it, stealing some damn ole TV, thinking he is a big shot. Bet the TV ain't no good either."

"You know Slick man, the brother is used to watching too much Sanford and Son."

"The brother got junk for brains, plain junk," [laughter]

Usually, convicts kept such conversations very short and always engage in them to make fun of someone else. Regularly, however, many would resort to coded language that only other convicts understand. Such manner of communication, reserved for prison trades and exchanges, sounds similar to the coded language utilized by Wall Street wheelers and dealers in their daily transactions.

CHAPTER 14
Prison Life After The Riots

Serving time behind the prison walls after the riot made me feel like a soldier in a rebel army. All of the black convicts, including myself, assumed African names. We considered ourselves a unit of the Black Nationalist movement. We followed the national news with keen interests, and behaved as we were part of the seventies radical movement. We read books such as; *Blood in My Eye* by George Jackson, *Soul on Ice* by Eldridge Cleaver, *If They Come for Me in The Morning* by Angela Davis, *The Red Book* by Mao Tse-Tung, and *The Green Book* by Kwame Nkrumah. Strange as it may seem, reading these radical works became a sort of self-discipline. Black convicts no longer sat around in anger, looking for ways to create small disturbances. Many consumed the radical literature which such interest that it left little time for provoking the prison guards.

Prior to being transferred to a medium security facility after the riot, I had filed a five hundred thousand dollar lawsuit for cruel and unusual punishment against the prison. For a while, I was absorbed in my own pretense of being an in-house convict-attorney. I read a lot of legal briefs, some I understood, some I didn't. I paid little attention to the legalese I did not understand, and made several false starts in preparing my case. Note book after note book, I filled with quotes and ideas. Gradually, in my own stupidity, I fancied myself a legal mind who could really take on the system. My expectations of success, and images of recognition, did not last long.

Months after filing my lawsuit, the Federal court honored my request to have my case heard. I took my seat in court gloating that I would finally have a chance to argue my case. "I can do it," I murmured to myself, "Junior you can do it." Before I could recollect my thoughts and listen to the judge's instructions, I heard the prosecutor saying, "Your Honor, the State will prove that this man (pointing directly at me) Ulyses B. Hooks was never mistreated … The State will further prove that Mr. Hooks has not been treated any worse than he had treated himself over the years." The prosecutor obviously had done his home work and found out that I was a substance abuser who lived in cars, streets and alleyways prior to my imprisonment. He narrated my past misgivings with great confidence, enunciating each incident as if he was there by my side living them with me. Each time he introduced a new arrest, he would look at me with a slight grin and turn to the judges to emphasize a number, *third … fourth* and so on. In this fashion he carried on for almost an hour. It was obvious that he felt good about his presentation, or might I say acting performance before the court. "He must have seen all the Perry Mason episodes on TV," I said to myself.

Upon hearing the prosecutor rake up my past misgivings, I felt hopeless. And, as he continued to lambaste my humanism, my hopelessness turned into anger. "How could the United States District court, who is our protector, allow this ridicule to go on?" I asked myself in disbelief. It is one thing to treat yourself cruel and unusual, but to have others do it to you against your will is unacceptable, I reasoned. My case was thrown out and I walked away from court feeling humiliated and depressed. "Was I treated this way because I was Black? Does my Blackness make me less human?" I pondered these questions for a while and came up with only one answer. That is, the inalienable rights of only some and not all people are guaranteed by the Constitution of the United States.

While serving time in prison, my father died. It was the greatest loss I ever suffered. News of my father's death reached me by way of my mother's phone call to the prison chaplain. I became broken hearted. I knew I would never see him again. I didn't have a chance to say goodbye. It is true that my father and I never had the best relationship. But what is a good father-son relationship, playing ball? Chatting? Hunting? I was never interested in these things and neither was my father. My father was a military man who did his best to provide for his family. He worked hard, days and nights. A man of few words, he had less than a handful of friends. His expression of fatherliness was not a textbook example of parent-child relationship. But, he loved his children. He shared their pains in his own way. He took pride in his military service and fighting for his country. Back home from war, he fought to support his family, to put food on the table instead of being dependent on public assistance programs. For a Black man in Oklahoma adequately supporting a family was quite a struggle. My father's affection towards me was not expressed in words but by the nightly peeks he took to make sure I had returned home from my daily drinking escapades. Hearing of his death, I cried myself to sleep that night. It was my loneliest of nights behind bars.

CHAPTER 15
Searching For Selfhood

In 1979, I received my release from prison after serving six and half years primarily at the Oklahoma State Penitentiary. For the first time, I was neither on probation nor indebted to the legal system. However, I had gained a new title. I became ex-convict Ulyses B. Hooks, Jr. The glorious taste of freedom was beyond belief. Being cooped up in a small cell, and conforming to the same daily routines distorts one's perspective on the value of human life. If prison was meant to reform or rehabilitate, it failed me. I walked away from a life behind bars feeling disoriented and disgraced. For the rest of my life, the label of ex-convict and the stigma it carries will return to haunt me as you will see in the pages that follow.

※ ※ ※

Prison, convicts are not taught what to expect when they return to a life in society. They are not socialized in accordance with the expectations, changing conditions and values of society. They are not sensitized to the stigma of being an ex-convict and how to cope with ostracism, yet they are expected to return to society as normal and productive citizens. The disorientation or dislocations suffered while imprisoned are considered the sole problems of the individual, which in some ways they are. Sometimes, however, no matter how hard the ex-convict tries to conform to the expectations of society, it is not he who determines the level or degree of accommodation and acceptance, it is the members of society that do so. And, most often the publics' response is rejection, thus penalizing the convict a second time for his past misdeeds. Prison does not cleanse the convict of his misdeeds; it only postpones for a short while, the indifference, the stigma and degradation he will have to face. I learned these truths after I left the Oklahoma State Penitentiary.

※ ※ ※

The day I walked out a freed man from the Oklahoma State Penitentiary, I felt a sense of relief. I had served my time. I wondered how the slaves must have felt when they gained their freedom. Were they overjoyed or sad, or were they like me, thinking about what the future has in store for them? Like them, I had no skills, no money, and in reality no home. With the death of my father, I knew things must have changed but in what ways, or by how much? I had no idea. I came of age behind prison walls, and all I possessed were the memories of years passed, a few pieces of clothes, and a few dollars in my pocket.

Stepping out into the sunlight, I marveled at the beauty of the outside world. Not that I hadn't seen the outside; I did almost daily. The difference this time was that I did not have to go back to a small cell to be counted and scrutinized like an inanimate object. My thoughts had changed because of my imprisonment. I was free to make choices. If I made them right, I would once again be transformed into being human. Gaining my release, I looked up into the sky and thanked God for delivering me from a world of confinement. With both hands, I shaded my eyes to scan the open skies. A flock of cranes flew by gracefully in silence. How beautiful, I thought. Lost in thoughts, a voice broke into my momentary peace, "Junior, Junior, hey Junior, I'm over here." It was my little sister. She was shouting to me and waiving her hands excitedly in order to gain my attention. She had driven the long journey to take me back home.

On our way back home, I spotted a street vendor and asked my sister to stop. I did not know why I asked her to stop at this particular junction. I got out of the car, and with the little money I had in my possession, I bought a little Buddha that sat on a pedestal. Before reaching home we veered off to visit my father's gravesite, and upon it I placed the Buddha. Years later, while I was away from home, my sister sent me a picture of my father's gravesite. There, in the photograph I could see - just above the tall grass, sat the Buddha against the backdrop of brilliant rays of light. So striking the image, one could swear that it is a depiction of enlightenment.

The six odd years I spent behind bars removed me from the realities of a changing world. I was six years older but six years behind the current realities. My perception of reality remained stuck at the time of my arrest. For me, time had stood still. I had to reorient myself to the external changes that had taken place during my incarceration. In looking at my younger brothers and sisters, I couldn't believe how much they had grown. Sadly, I felt estranged from them. They no longer needed me to braid their hair or settle their disputes. During my absence they became young men and women. Listening to them talk among themselves made me feel like a stranger in their midst. I was among them, yet not with them. Not that they shunned me or ignored my presence; it was just that they interacted with me differently than they did with each other. They were thinking prospectively and I, retrospectively. I spoke about their past, their conversations focused on the future. Painfully, I tried to invent new ways to reconnect with them and reintegrate with the family. My efforts failed.

❧ ❧ ❧

Prison does not prepare a convict for life away from prison. In fact, incarceration robs the prisoner of his enduring connections, instills distrust and fashions new modes of survival based on a sort of solitary individualism. I find it interesting when people in general, and academicians in particular, make pronouncements about reintegrating ex-convicts into the family and society. Many of these individuals never spent a single day behind prison walls. They have not experienced the loneliness, the alienation and the fear of every day existence caused by incarceration. I remember once in one of my criminology graduate courses a guest speaker spent over an hour pontificating about reintegration into the family and how this is crucial for successful rehabilitation of ex-convicts. Throughout the hour, I heard about the need for individual counseling and other forms of therapy, and things the family can do to make rehabilitation successful. The speaker made no mention of the of ex-convicts warped sense of reality, the contradistinctions in prison and societal relations, and how these hinder reintegration. Furthermore, the speaker failed to address the social and legal stigmas of imprisonment, the lack of labor market preparedness and ex-convicts low level of education, all of which hinder reintegration into the family and society.

❧

CHAPTER 16
Coming To Washington D.C.

Reintegration into my family proved more difficult than I had envisioned so I had to find a way out. With the passing of my father, my mother found herself a male friend. His presence around her filled me with anxiety and resentment. As time passed, I became increasingly irritable whenever I saw him. Suspecting that my relationship with my mother's friend would soon be confrontational, my younger brother called from Washington, D.C., and invited me to go and live with him for a while. It did not take long for me to make my decision. I had no job, no skills, no money; what did I have to lose? I was going nowhere fast in Oklahoma City. So I accepted my brother's invitation. Borrowing money from my sister, I purchased a bus ticket and the very next day I set out on my journey to the U.S Capitol.

Arriving in Washington, D.C., I thought I had discovered freedom. Stepping off the bus, I looked in all directions to absorb life in the big city. People bustled everywhere.

Noise, and the aroma of different foods, filled the air. The smell of food made me feel quite hungry, but with little money in my pocket, I had to resist the temptation of spending on a big meal. I bought a slice of pizza from a vendor in the bus station, picked up my bag and started walking to find my brother's apartment. He and his wife had rented an efficiency condo-apartment in Foggy Bottom. Knowing that I would be unable to find his apartment without guidance, my brother provided me with the necessary directions before I left Oklahoma.

Foggy Bottom stood some distance away from the bus station so I decided to take my time and observe the neighborhoods as I walked on. In some respects, Washington D.C., reminded me of some of the areas I traveled in California. The ceaseless street activities, the vendors and the bums, the elites and the working class, the trashy buildings and the mansions, all converge and diverge in an endless array of poverty and wealth. Having walked some distance in silence, I tried to whistle but no sound came through my lips. I then tried to sing softly to myself but I sounded horrible. I stopped as soon as I started lest someone hear my vocal grunts. Taking a quick glance around, and finding no one within ear shot, I smiled at myself for sounding like a tone deaf frog. Suddenly, I recalled how I faked my chorus lines the time my elementary school teacher took us to the radio station to perform. This made me laugh a little louder.

Leisurely walking for some time, I came to my brother's apartment. Ringing the door bell, my brother opened the door and greeted me with a big hug. He seemed quite happy to see me. He asked about my life in prison, and empathized when I told him how lonely I felt being away from the family. Talking to my brother helped me to relieve some of my post-prison stress.

Imprisonment takes a toll on the human psyche, creating deep scars which come to light after the individual is no longer confined. I was to experience the discombobulation caused by imprisonment several times over, during my journey in and out of homelessness.

Residing with my brother and his wife in their tiny apartment turned out to be a daily game of hide and seek. Management regulations prohibited any additional person living in the apartment. By allowing me to live with them, my brother and his wife were in violation of their lease agreement. If caught, we would all be evicted. In order not to be seen by the neighbors or apartment personnel, I had to sneak in and out of the building. Each day, I would slip away early in the morning and return after dark, trying my utmost not to be detected. This pattern of hide and seek continued for the entire period I lived with my brother.

My first days in D.C., I spent walking around viewing the monuments of the great city. It seemed as if everything that I had studied in school came to life, everything except the intense misery of some of D.C's, inhabitants. In my walks through downtown, I passed numerous homeless people, most of them Black. Little did I realize at the time that I would one day join their midst. Each day, as I journeyed through the streets, I could sense the despair among the homeless Blacks, some eating out of garbage cans, some living in the park in front of the Whitehouse, and one lying on the Capitol steps. "Is this the real Washington, D.C.?" I asked myself. I never read about this in my school books, or heard about it from my teachers.

At nights, back in my brother's apartment, I spent many hours reflecting on my strolls around town. Frequently, my reflections left me feeling despondent. All of my life I viewed Washington, D.C., as the protector of mankind. And, of all places on earth, I envisioned it to be a city where people were treated with dignity and respect. I saw little of these things in the streets. In fact, the misery I saw haunted me. It also prompted me to re-examine my own situation.

⁂ ⁂ ⁂

As street life in Washington D. C, played out in my mind, I wondered, sometimes aloud, and sometimes in silence, about the demise of the street people. At times, I also wondered about my own predicament. Rationally, or irrationally, I came to the conclusion that the district court in Oklahoma City railroaded me to prison, that the Constitutional rights of Black men amounted to a big joke. I was just another Black man, like the hundreds living in the streets. From that point on, I felt lost. I didn't know what to do, or where to go. Nothing seemed to matter anymore. It dawned on me, that if you became a victim of the system, it was solely your own fault. And if it wasn't, it would be proven as such, especially if you were poor, or Black. The justice system is never seen to be in error. And here in Washington, D.C., there seems to be no justice. In the city of fairness, unfairness predominated, in the city of the affluent, poverty rules the day, especially in the alleys, streets and boulevards; two distinct worlds commingling daily in a rhythmic flow of opposites.

⁂ ⁂ ⁂

Living in D.C., for a few weeks, I went to work selling Indian jewelry for a street-vendor whom I met through my brother. Peddling started out as fun, and allowed me to meet many interesting people. Sadly for me, it turned out less profitable than I thought. Many days, I hardly made enough for lunch and cigarettes. Street vending, however, allowed me to sharpen my intellectual skills. People from all walks of life came to my table. The majority willingly shared their opinions about any and everything. The wide ranging topics included the mundane, such as the weather, to the profound, such as the effects of congressional political and economic policies on the nation. Believe me, there is no political encounter like that of Washington, D.C. Within a short while, I became convinced that if you want to know the real state of the Union, just ask a D.C., native.

Life's journey is often fraught with twists and turns and mine was no different. While living with my brother, he asked me to accompany him to one of his Scientology seminars that he taught. Up until then, I had not given much thought much about my own Spirituality. Railroaded by the criminal justice system, which leaves the poor person stigmatized for life, I began to question the Divine, and soon thereafter seemed to have lost faith. My brother's invitation at first did not appeal to me, but I decided to accompany him anyway. He was kind to let me live with him, hence I felt that I should reciprocate by accepting his invitation. To my surprise, I found the Scientology discourse quite enlightening. The focus on self awareness and self actualization appealed to me. Personal problems, I felt, could be solved through self examination, and analyses of the distractions. The external turbulences that hinder the promotion of internal happiness could be minimized through the realization of the true self. From thereon, I became a believer, and took it upon myself to explore the philosophy in some detail.

CHAPTER 17
Marriage And Separation

I was getting accustomed to life in D.C., when my bother and his Mauritian wife decided to leave for an extended vacation to Mauritius. Married for a few months, they decided to take a trip to the wife's home country to visit with her relatives. Knowing that I would be unable to financially upkeep their apartment during their absence, they decided sublease. For days I wondered how I would survive after they leave. Then, I decided that I could get married to Judy, a girl I had met a few weeks earlier.

Walking down "M" street in Georgetown one night, I stopped to listen to a musician playing a John Coltrane tune on his saxophone. A young Black woman and her friend came up and joined me; her name was Judy. Without hesitation, I introduced myself to them. We then talked and listened to the music for a while. Getting ready to leave, the girls offered me a ride home. I accepted.

Judy and I dated several times after that first meeting. She loved cheesecake. On occasions, we went to the "Blue Mirror", a place famous for its cheesecake in D.C. At the time, Judy was in the Air Force Reserve, and worked at Andrew's Air Force base in Camp Springs, Maryland. She told me that her military superiors once offered her a position on Air Force One, the President's plane. I was impressed. Dating Judy gave me hope. I learned a lot about her family and she learned about mine. From Judy, I found out that her father was a Prince Hall mason. I didn't have a relationship with him before, or after meeting his daughter. I did learn, however, that he was angry with me for marrying his daughter without his consent. Like so many incidences in my life, the marriage just happened.

One day, on the brink of becoming homeless, Judy and I decided to get married. Armed with a marriage license, we knocked on a preacher's door, showed him the license, and he gladly pronounced us husband and wife. The moment we stepped out of the preacher's house it started to rain. Loud clapping of the thunder and frightening displays of lightening accompanied the heavy downpour of rain. Perhaps it was nature's omen that our union would not survive. Several days after the marriage, we told Judy's family. Reluctantly, they accepted us. Neither Judy's mom nor her dad gave us their blessings.

After marriage, Judy and I moved into a one-bedroom apartment in Northeast, D.C., close to the Rhode Island Avenue subway stop. Since I didn't have a job, I stuck around the apartment until Judy left for work; I then went in search of any type of employment I could find. For an ex-convict with only a G.E.D, employment did not come about easily.

Potential employers customarily asked for previous work experience, and mine was extremely limited. How does someone acquire work experience while serving time in prison? Prison is not a training school that prepares convicts for jobs in the labor force. Some convicts do acquire skills such as brick layers, masons, carpenters, upholsterers, etc., while imprisoned but, not every prisoner has such opportunities.

Each morning, before making my rounds of job hunting, I walked Judy to the subway station as if I was there to protect her. Needless to say, Judy didn't need my protection. As a matter of fact, given her military training, and employment in the Air Force, she could protect herself better than me, from any intruder. In military uniform, Judy looked striking and confident, and I admired her with a taint of jealousy. Occasionally, I wondered how she truly felt about me, but dismissed the thoughts as fast as thy entered my mind for fear that I may find myself unworthy of her.

Judy treated our marriage with great sensitivity, and her reactions toward me were sort of angelic. She agreed to marry me knowing of my circumstances as I stood on the precipice of homelessness. She gave much, and asked for very little in return. Like clockwork, every morning, she would leave me enough money to get a couple quarts of beer, and a pack of cigarettes. She did not probe my soul searching for evil intentions. She shared my thoughts and encouraged me to chase after my dream of turning my prison poems into a publishable manuscript. In retrospect, I realize that working on the poems kept me in prison even though I was free.

Imprisoned for over six years had shackled my mind, and I could not extricate my inner Self from such mental bondage. Judy might have realized the turbulence in my tormented Soul, and knew she could not help me to relinquish my past. After ninety days of marriage, we separated. To this day, I still can't identify the things that drove Judy and I apart, except for my mental bondage, and the fact that I had no future. My past incarceration kept me imprisoned in current day tormented Soul.

❧

CHAPTER 18
Homeless In D.C.

Explanations abound as to why some people become homeless. Among the most noted explanations is that homeless people are a bunch of lazy losers who do not want to work for a living. More times than I can count, I have heard people say that the homeless population is nothing more than a bunch of lazy winos, bums and derelicts, the scum of society. While such labels may be applicable to some in the homeless population, everyone can not be characterized as such. Being homeless for a greater part of my life, I have found that those who make up the homeless population originated from all walks of life. Among the homeless people are individuals who were once successful professionals, fathers, mothers, college graduates, illiterates, sane, insane and the poor, some of whom experienced poverty since childhood. As I have lived and seen it from within and without, the homeless population is an amalgam of fabled princes and paupers.

For me, the break-up of my marriage with Judy ushered in the second coming of my long battle with homelessness. In late 1979, I left the apartment that Judy and I had shared to live on the streets of the District of Columbia. I had nowhere else to go. My pride, and my past, stood in the way of achieving the American dream. As I moved out into the streets to join the ranks of homeless, I quickly realized that in the greatest capital of the world, resided a sub-society of people who gathered together primarily at night only to be dispersed as homeless individuals at the crack of dawn. The monuments, subway stops, alley ways, and park benches, amidst the garbage and burnt out buildings, the homeless gather temporarily each night to constitute and reconstitute their sub-society. They do so unconcerned about the colors or dispositions of their neighbors. On any given night, they could be seen climbing in and out of dumpsters behind the fast food restaurants, sliding into cardboard boxes in alleys. And in the winter, they could be seen standing on steam grates to keep warm. I became one of them, unknown and unnoticed in their overcrowded midst.

The degradation I had to undergo as a homeless individual in D.C., is hard to explain in words. At times, I thought I would never survive. For the sake of staying alive I had to beg, and prepare myself for insults and ridicule. Little did I realize that along the way, the degrading and humiliating circumstances desensitize the individual over time. Slowly, the insults and ridicule became a part of my daily expectations.

I remained homeless in the streets of Washington, D.C., until I could no longer withstand the daily sufferings. About to lose my mind, I decided to hitchhike home.

Back in Oklahoma, I managed to get a job working as an underground cable installer. With the money I saved from working, I bought a car. Owning a car enabled me to travel to and from work with pride. It also allowed me to frequent the bars and night clubs during the evenings. One night, driving home after drinking at one of the bars, I was stopped and charged with drunken driving. With no legal representation, I pleaded guilty and served six months in jail. Shortly after getting out of jail, Judy, my ex-wife called to say that I had a daughter, and that if I wanted to see her, I had to return D.C. It didn't take long for me to decide. Elated at the news, and anxious to see my daughter, I once again took a bus ride back to D.C.

Arriving in D.C., my life got off to an excellent start. I stayed with Judy and her sister. They both treated me with kindness and respect. During this time, I did my utmost to bond with my daughter. I took her out for walks in her stroller, and played made-up games with her as I took short rests on benches in the park and on street corners. Given my previous experience in helping to raise my little brothers and sisters, taking care of my daughter came with much ease. I was already an expert at changing diapers and wiping runny noses. Observing my daughter's little hands and feet jerk upwards into the air filled my heart with joy. And when she smiled at my "coos" and "ooz", my heart would beat with special pride for she was a part of me, and me of her. Today, I can still see her toothless gum as she broke into her bright smiles and my heart would sink. I was not there to see her take her first steps, hear her first words, or contribute to her well being. Not long after I arrived in D.C., my life took a turn for the worse. Things started to fall apart after Judy repeatedly rebuffed my requests to reconcile with her. I knew then I had to leave in due course.

In order to be close to my daughter, and help in rearing her, I got a job at a pizza parlor. My responsibilities included cleaning the place and preparing it for opening in the mornings. The first few days I worked like a pro. Then, I started pilfering from the stock of wine and beers which the parlor also sold. Knowing that Judy would not reconcile with me despite my pleas, I began to drink heavily, increasing my consumption with each day. To avoid being detected as the pilferer, I would leave the pizza parlor early in the morning before the manager arrived. This cat-and-mouse game worked for a few days, but good things don't last. My drinking must have put a dent on the parlor's profit for the manger started taking daily account of his stock. It didn't take long for him to discover the true identity of the pilferer, and thereupon he fired me.

Soon after being fired, I found out that my brother and his wife had returned to D.C., I left Judy and her sister's apartment determined to make it on my own. Turning to my brother for assistance, I found out that the apartment building where he and his wife lived would not allow me to stay with them. To enforce the rental policies, management hired security guards to make sure guests came and left as per the lease. My brother, therefore, could not accommodate me. I had to fend for myself. Once again, I relied on the D.C., underground for survival. For some time, I slept in my brother's taxi in the alleys, and on occasion, in the homeless shelter. The shelter in D.C. turned out to be the most dangerous place for the homeless. There was no law enforcement authority present in, or around the building.

Everyone seemed to be operating under the principle of an eye for an eye, a tooth for a tooth. Fights and stabbings took place frequently without any intervention by the law enforcement authority.

The nights I slept at the D.C., shelter, I spent more time awake than asleep. The fear of being stabbed or strangled to death rested heavily on my mind. The homeless group did not care about individual rights. In their world, there was no such thing as *rights*. From what I observed, the homeless knew they were not a respected group. Why then must they show respect for others. Many homeless individuals live for the day, unconcerned about tomorrow. Trust was not something they had in common. They came together at nights to catch a few hours of sleep, not to make friends or influence scoundrels. In their crowded gatherings, they considered themselves single individuals with changing identities. The anger built up in them during the day's efforts to survive manifested itself with the slightest provocation. Some times, a mere look can trigger a fight. I made it my rule not to provoke anyone. This became my first lesson in homelessness, and I still abide by it today.

CHAPTER 19
Homeless In New York City

After a series of hardships, my homelessness in D.C., became quite burdensome. Acting on an impulse, I hitched my way to New York City. All of my life, I wanted to live in New York, and there I arrived, finally.

Unlike D.C., I quickly discovered the people of New York to be quite friendly. For a few days, I hung out in the streets drinking cheap beers and wines with some of New York's homeless. Shortly thereafter, I became acquainted with a group of homeless I had met in Tompkins Square Park. Together, we illegally occupied an abandoned apartment on Avenue B, on the lower eastside of Manhattan. Apparently, New York City had a policy that if you homesteaded in an abandoned apartment for an extended period, the city would not evict you unless it found you a livable apartment. For my homeless buddies and me, Avenue B became our secret haven.

Within the span of a few weeks of living in New York City, I managed to drink and drug all over Manhattan. Forty Second Street became one of my favorite jaunts; I hung out there practically every day. One day, filled with drugs and alcohol, I staggered through Forty Second and Eighth Avenue, and was struck down by a taxi. Unconscious, an ambulance took me to Saint Luke's Roosevelt hospital. As the nurses wheeled me into the operating room, I regained consciousness. The attending doctor immediately asked for my identification. I took out my wallet and showed him my Washington, D.C., driver's license. Looking at it for a split second, the doctor handed it back to me and told me I could go. I knew he needed proof of health insurance, and I had none. Being a homeless addict, where would I get health insurance?

I left the hospital in unbearable pain. My boots, pants, and shirt were cut in a manner that would have enabled the nurses to strip me on the operating table. The doctor determined that I didn't need any medical attention and forced me to leave with my clothes hanging all over me. In my tattered clothes, I must have looked like the incredible hulk after his anger subsided, but I didn't care. Somehow, I managed to drag myself to 14th street where I bought a pair of thongs from a street vendor. Seeing my physical condition, a passerby stopped and told me to go to the Volunteer's of America shelter on Wards Island. He must have been a *Guardian Angel* for he appeared out of nowhere to direct me to a place where I would stay for over five months.

When I arrived at the Wards Island shelter, the attendant greeted me with courtesy, gave me food, and a bed which I occupied throughout my stay there. Over the months, the shelter taught me a few things about the life of poor New Yorkers. During winter, many of the poor, denied adequate heat, gave up their apartments for the warmth of the shelter. This, they did, because their landlords refused to keep their buildings warm. According to them, the landlords complained about the high cost of heating the buildings. Residents at the shelter included Vietnam veterans, drug addicts, alcoholics, homosexuals, elderly, unwed mothers, and even people with nine to five jobs. The Wards Island shelter represented a melting pot of New York's underclass. The shelter offered everyone a bed, for as long as they wanted it; three meals a day, and bus tokens for daily travel to and from Manhattan.

The atmosphere at the Wards Island shelter was a far cry from the homeless shelter in Washington D.C. At the D.C., shelter chaos reigned; discourtesy and mistrust were the norms of everyday operation. At the Wards Island shelter, order, trust and courtesy prevailed. The people who stayed there were friendly, willingly assisted those in need, and seldom used foul language when conversing with each other. I lived there until I recuperated.

While living at the Wards Island shelter, I met a man who peddled advertisement for a personal injury attorney. He gave me one of the lawyer's business cards and I went to see him. The lawyer took my case and a few weeks later gave me eleven hundred dollars as my part of the settlement. It was the largest sum of money I have had in a long time. For safe keep, I opened up a savings account. Every morning, I would go to the bank and withdraw enough money to drink and drug for the entire day. One day, with some of the money I withdrew, I went to a thrift store in Harlem and bought some new clothes. I was beginning to feel a sense of self worth.

Prior to receiving the settlement money, I met a guy who wanted to go into the silk screening business, printing T-shirts. We got together, purchased the printing equipment, and began producing silk-screened T-shirts out of his Spanish Harlem apartment. The guy did the silk screening, and I sold the shirts. I was all over New York: the Village, the Westside, the lower Eastside, little Italy, So-Ho, No-Ho, the Bowery, and Harlem. I peddled shirts in and out of Marcus Garvey Park, up and down 125th street. I visited the National Black Theatre and several other notable places in Harlem. To say the least, Harlem indeed looked like a cultural Mecca at the time.

CHAPTER 20
Back To D.C Where I Met An Angel

The business of peddling T-shirts did not bring any financial gains. And, since I was running out of money, I decided to leave New York. One day, I bought a bus ticket to D.C. Afterwards, I went to a thrift shop in Harlem and purchased a pair of Fry boots that I had seen in the display window. Decked out in a black blazer, white shirt and tie, grey trousers, and the tan Fry boots, I took the subway to Forty Second Street to catch the Greyhound bus to D.C. On my way coming up out of the subway, I lost one of the heels of my Fry boots. I searched for a shoe shop to get the boot repaired, but found all of them closed. Not wanting to miss my bus, I threw the boots away and bought a pair of thongs. I then bought a six-pack of sixteen ounce Old English 800 malt liquor, drank them all, and boarded the bus bounded for D.C.

In D.C., I once again took to the streets for a couple of days, wearing the black blazer, grey trousers, white shirt and tie, and thongs. People took a second glance when they saw me. I must have looked ridiculous in my outfit.

One evening, tired and hungry, I stumbled into the courtyard of St. Paul's Episcopal Church, and stood in line to get a sandwich. Ruth, an Irish female with flaming red hair, looked at me standing there in my black blazer, gray trousers, dirty white shirt and tie, and thongs waiting to get a sandwich. Like the many passersby, she too must have thought I looked quite ridiculous, but she showed no signs of it. With utmost politeness, she approached me and asked, "What brought you to church today?"

Without putting much thought into my response, I said:

"I am a writer and am down on my luck."

"Where are you coming from?"

"New York City," I replied.

Whether Ruth was amused, I couldn't tell for she asked her questions with such earnestness she made me feel worthy.

"How long would you be in D.C?" she asked.

"I am not sure."

"Come see us again soon," Ruth said as she went on to greet others standing in the food line.

From my first encounter with Ruth, I felt as if I had entered into a spiritual journey. She spoke to me with such kindness she made me feel like a true human being. She did not laugh at the way I looked, or seem amused when I told her I was writer and down on my luck. She listened with politeness and grace, and offered her help. Because of Ruth, I regularly showed up at St. Paul's. Gradually, she accepted me as a friend. Knowing that I drank, she occasionally gave me a few dollars for beers. Once, when I was drunk, she opened the door to the church hall thereby sparing me from having to sleep in the cold street.

I started attending morning mass with Ruth, and ate breakfast with her group afterwards. Ruth always packed a bag of lunch for me to take when I leave. And, when she could afford it, she gave me a couple of dollars. During her workdays, I walked her to the "State Department" where she was employed, say goodbye and return to my daily routine of coffee, doughnuts, and a drink. Afterwards, I would go to the Martin Luther King Jr. (MLK) memorial library to read. The MLK library had virtually turned into a homeless shelter. It was as if Martin Luther King Jr. had ordained it so.

As a result of relationship with Ruth, I made the decision to be baptized one Easter Sunday and become a member of St. Paul's Episcopal Church. To help me get my life together, my Godfather assisted me in obtaining a job as a shipping clerk. In giving me the job, my employer entrusted me with the keys to the executive bathroom. This made me feel trustworthy. The pay was good and I took my responsibilities seriously. With my steady income, I started on a new life course. Ruth assisted me in obtaining an apartment. Having some semblance of stability, I ushered in church every third Sunday, kissed the bishop's ring after confirmation, and prayed to God that I would stay the course of reform. This task proved more difficult than I imagined. Behavioral change came slowly. With money in my pocket, I began to drink more, and occasionally inject cocaine. I had a good job with good pay and a nice apartment in Foggy

Bottom, but I kept sliding back into the behavioral gutter. Because of my drinking, I lost my job after three years.

Shortly thereafter, Ruth paid my way to taxi school. I then started driving a taxi thinking I could recuperate from my downward spiral. This turned out to be a mistake. Driving a taxi gave me access to all the illicit drug houses in D.C. Addicted to drugs and alcohol, I fell behind in paying my rent. I went to the church only when I needed someone to bail me out. At first, no one asked any questions. With each passing day, I sank deeper and deeper into addiction and hopelessness. Sensing my unwillingness or inability to reform, the priest one day said to me, "I think its time for you to leave town and see if you could turn your life around." I was crushed. When a priest tells you it is time to leave town, it had to be that some adversities forced him to such a decision.

My first thought about the priest's suggestion focused on how much I must have disappointed Ruth. Ruth had served as my *Guardian Angel*. She taught me the love of mankind, or should I say womankind. Her actions and teachings helped me to acknowledge the authenticity of her spirituality, as well as that of others. She fed me when I had no food, clothed me when I came close to being naked, and found me a place to lay my head when I had nowhere to bed. She assisted me when illness overtook my body and soul, and gave me comfort. In spite of her concerns, love and assistance, I couldn't pull myself up from sliding down the homeless path.

CHAPTER 21
Oklahoma Here I Come Again

Addiction afflicts millions of Americans from all walks of life. Most often, addicts of poor backgrounds are quite visible because they can be seen wandering the streets. Wealthy addicts are seldom seen, and regularly heard about after completing treatment at high cost centers that only they can afford.

I am not among the fortunate. I wish I understood the part in me that craved for drugs and alcohol. Some may say that this is just an excuse, but it is my Truth. Today, I am drug and alcohol free, and have been so for nearly six years. What made me stop drinking and drugging I am not sure; but I wish I knew how to extricate my self from the downward spiral of addiction much earlier. Had I known how to do so, I would not have disappointed my family, my wife and child, my pastor and most of all Ruth.

Some times, when I close my eyes, I can still see Ruth trying to make sense of my addiction. She believed in me, but I didn't believe in myself. She invested in me, she prayed with me and she encouraged me to take charge of my life, but I failed her at every step of the way. It must have disappointed her to see me fall back into a life of decadence and degradation. She was truly an angel in my homeless path, and although she did not succeed in reforming me, she triggered my moral conscience which I would come to realize much later in life.

❧ ❧ ❧

Running out of safe havens in D.C., I took the priest's words to heart, licked my wounds and moved back to Oklahoma City. Having lived in D.C., and New York City, life in Oklahoma quickly turned into a drab. Once again, I turned to alcohol and drugs, squandering my opportunities, and letting everyone down who had tried to help me. Somehow, I just couldn't get it right.

One good that resulted from my return to Oklahoma was the completion of my manuscript of poems. With high hopes, I mailed it off to a publisher whose address I found in the newspapers. Within two weeks the publisher wrote back praising my manuscript, and presenting me with a plan to get it published. The plan required me to send him six thousand four hundred and eighty dollars. He would publish thirty five hundred copies, and promote me on the television and radio stations that I desired any where in the country. The letter ended by saying, "Now go out and find someone that believes in you."

After reading the letter, I embarked on a mission of getting someone to fund me. I called my paternal uncle asking for his support. He gave me a million reasons why he couldn't grant me any. My uncle's rejection made me feel dejected. How could he refuse me, his own flesh and blood? Is it because he didn't want to see me succeed? Was he jealous? These questions raced through my mind, and impacted my ability to reason things rationally. Rereading the publisher's letter, I realized that I had failed to grasp its subtlety. Finding someone to believe in me was literally impossible given the life that I had lived. No one in Oklahoma would risk a dime on me, not even a blood relative.

❧

CHAPTER 22
A Journey To Nowhere

Wallowing in my state of hopelessness, my baby sister said to me that she was moving back to Denver, Colorado. I asked if I could ride with her out of town and she agreed. I reasoned that I could determine what to do with my life as I rode along with her. I had communicated with Gwendolyn Brooks (the Black female poet laureate of Illinois) while I was in prison, and decided to go to Chicago to meet her. The problem, however, was how to get there. In traveling to Denver, I didn't realize how far away from Chicago I would be until my sister let me off at a truck stop on the outskirts of Denver. Parting from her was sad. She gave me five dollars to get me something to eat, and then said, "Goodbye Junior, good luck and take care." Thus began my long journey to Chicago.

Standing by the roadside with my thumb up, the driver an eighteen-wheeler stopped to give me a ride on the condition that I help him unload his truck when we got inside of Denver. The route he took was quick, and passed under a bridge on which airplanes landed. I had never seen anything like this before, planes and trucks crisscrossing not far from each other. After unloading the truck we headed out of Denver, on our way to Wheat Ridge, Colorado. I got off at Wheat Ridge and tried to hustle another ride with no success.

After three days of sleeping on the ground in and around the truck stop, I caught a ride on a Mayflower moving van going to Albuquerque, New Mexico, and later to Arizona. Three of us rode on this long tiresome drive. To ease our discomforts somewhat, the driver provided the food, and all the beer we could drink. In return, he asked that we unload the truck when we reached the destinations. Rolling into Albuquerque, a sky filled with hot air balloons greeted us. Later, we found out that it was the beginning of the balloon festival. Upon delivering our load in Albuquerque, we took a short rest and then headed out to Arizona.

In Arizona, after we unloaded the truck, I left the Mayflower crew to find transportation onward. Leaving Arizona proved to be quite challenging. Unable to resist the street life of Phoenix, I started drinking with the natives. This delayed my journey for a couple of days. During the day, I drank; at nights, I slept at the homeless shelter. Phoenix was unique in that it had an outdoor shelter where the homeless people put up makeshift tents in an enclosed area behind the main shelter building. From what I observed, the tent-shelters proved to be a lawless place for homeless people. Under these makeshift tents, the homeless drank and drugged in plain view of the public. Somewhat similar to the D.C, shelter, the Phoenix shelter was a boisterous place, but without the intense distrust among the homeless crowd.

I had only spent a few days in Phoenix when the cops arrested me for begging. Released from jail the next day, I decided to get out of town, and hitched a ride with a truck driver on his way to Los Angeles. In Los Angeles, I applied for and received food stamps. Following standard street practices of the time, I traded the food stamps for money. With the money received from the trade, I purchased a bus ticket to Las Vegas. In my view, Las Vegas could be likened to a prison with laws and regulations to control everything except gambling. Regulations prohibited panhandling, and people there refused to give monetary assistance to anyone in the streets, even the neediest. The unwritten assumption seemed to be that everyone there was out to get easy money. Even the welfare system of Vegas displayed an unwillingness to assist those who were legitimately stranded.

Down on my luck, I hopped on a freight train going to Salt Lake City Utah. I was happy to be on my way out of Las Vegas. Happiness, however, soon turned into misery. Riding the train in the dead of winter, I almost froze to death during the eighteen-hour train journey. I prayed non-stop for my safe deliverance. I prayed in so many ways, I can hardly count. Had I known ten different languages, I would have prayed in all of them, hoping that God would at least understand one. It is strange how a person often appeals to God in times of crisis. I dozed off praying, only to find myself awakened and still praying. In my transfixed state of mind between sleep and wake, I felt as if I was drawn closer to God. It was He who kept me sane and alive at a time when I had given up all hopes of survival.

I jumped off of the train near the Union Pacific train yard in Salt Lake City, which to my surprise, happened to be near the Rescue mission. Already numb from the cold train ride, I stepped out into falling snow flakes as big as my thumb. They were the biggest snow flakes I had ever seen, and they came at a time when I was already half frozen, thereby adding to my misery. With much effort, I made it to the door of the mission. The guy who opened the door informed me that it was too late to get a bed, but seeing my condition, relented and gave me a bed. Over a period of days, I recuperated with the help of cheap wine and beer. Feeling fit to move on my feet again, I went to the welfare office, applied for financial assistance and food stamps, and received both. Instead of moving on, I stayed in Salt Lake City drinking and drugging until my last check and food stamps. Somehow, I managed to buy a ticket, and set out on my way to San Diego, California.

The second time around in San Diego things looked much different than the first. I managed to drink and drug the entire time I stayed there. Unable to escape the long arms of the law, I got a ticket for sleeping on the sidewalk. I then went and lived under the Coronado Bridge. To survive, I turned to the San Diego welfare system which gave me food stamps and a check. As usual, I drank and drugged until my last check, and then bought a bus ticket to Chicago.

Drunk and filthy, I joined the bus in San Diego bounded for Chicago. I do not remember much of the journey except that it took a very long time to come to an end. Being drunk most of the journey, I paid little attention to anything. As the bus pulled into stations where the stops lasted for an hour or more, I would rush to the nearest available store, buy a couple of beers and guzzle them down before we took off again. In this fashion, I lost track of time, and thus escaped the boredom that usually resulted from such long trips. The only thing I do recall from the journey is the brightness of the full moon which accompanied us during the final hours of our ride. I interpreted it to be a good sign, and wished that it would bring me some success.

CHAPTER 23
Searching From Chicago To D.C

I arrived in Chicago during the drought of the eighties. At the time many people considered it a fun city and flocked there. Shortly after stepping off the bus, I applied for welfare and food stamps, and received these after a few days. To cope, I sought comfort in different homeless shelters. One shelter in particular had an armed guard because the home-less men became unruly at times.

Upon receiving the welfare checks, I moved into a single room occupancy (SRO) hotel on State Street. My new found happiness, however, did not last very long. Arrested for beg-ging, and afraid of going back to jail, I left Chicago and went to Milwaukee. In Milwaukee, I felt trapped. Unable to obtain a check or food stamps because of the prolonged application process, I became desperate to leave the city. Inquiring into assistance, a few people guided me to some community advocates. I went to them and told them that I was trying to get a bus ticket to Washington, D.C. They told me that if someone would guarantee that I would have a place to live when I got there, they would get me a ticket. I gave them the number of an acquaintance who agreed to their conditions. Satisfied that I would find a place to stay in D.C., the advocates gave me a ticket and drove me to the bus station. I guess it was their way of making sure that I would not sell the bus ticket and squander the money. The bus ride from Milwaukee turned out to be miserable for I was sober all of the way.

I was glad when I arrived in D.C., feeling quite happy because I could find ways to get a drink. My only set back was finding a place to stay other than the homeless shelter. Afraid of the shelter's conditions, I contacted a guy named Michael who had farms for alcoholics in Alderson, West Virginia. I happened to know Michael from my previous visit to D.C. He was like the male "Mother Teresa" of D.C. I arranged with Michael to be picked up at a designated location, and he drove me to one of his farms in West Virginia. He had already purchased three farms from West Virginia farmers, many of whom experienced great economic hardships at the time. Michael bought farms for top dollar with the money people donated toward his cause of helping the poor. Within a short period, Michael's farms became a haven for D.C., alcoholics.

Most establishments have rules, and Michael's farms were no different, except that Michael's rules seemed like non-rules. Simply summed they appeared to say: *You didn't have to do anything you didn't feel like doing.* During my short stay, I took this interpretation of the rules to heart. I didn't do anything except to write poems and make inquires into finding someone who would back me financially to get them published.

The farm where I lived sat on a mountain top. When it rained, you needed a four-wheel-drive vehicle to get up or down the mountain. At nights it was pitch black; you couldn't even see your hand in front of your face. When it snowed, it covered all the pathways leading to the farm, except for the freshly made tracks left by the roaming animals. In the winter, we used a wood-burning stove to heat the place. The toilet was outside which made our comings and goings less frequent. To keep the stove burning, we had to cut our own wood. Since I seldom assisted with the chores, Michael asked me to leave just after a brief stay. I am not sure whether the other residents complained about me, but one day Michael came in and told me to leave. He offered to buy me a bus ticket to wherever I wanted to go. I chose New York. Not long after, I was once again on my way to the Big Apple.

CHAPTER 24
Back To New York Where I Met An Angel

Manhattan, to me, was a substance abuser's paradise. Drugs and alcohol could be purchased at anytime, night or day, and for cheap or dear. Like it is today, Manhattan downtown never slept. Constant activities filled the air. In operation all night, the subway provided cheap transportation, and served as a temporary sanctuary for numerous homeless addicts all over the city. Regularly, early subway travelers found themselves face to face with the homeless addicts still on the train, all trying to shake off their lack of sleep. I was one of such addicts. Over a period of time, I graduated from sleeping on the train to sleeping in The Port Authority, home of the commercial buses, and the converging point for many trains. Each morning, I would join the throng of homeless addicts in the Port Authority bathrooms, awaiting my turn to wash my face and brush my teeth. Physically filthy from hours of drinking and drugging, my visits to the bathrooms became my ritual of daily cleansing.

Tired of panhandling, I started vending Bart Simpson T-shirts, tube socks, yo-yos, model cars, and batteries on the floor of The Port Authority, using the little money I saved. Vending gave me some independence and enabled me to make enough money to support my addictive drug and alcohol habits. At the end of each day, I took stock of my earnings and depending on my profit, purchased small quantities of marijuana and beers to last me late into the night.

New Years celebration of 1989 happened to be my best night in Manhattan. Early that evening, people began crowding into Times Square in preparation of the dropping of the ball. Within a few hours, the place became so crowded people stood cheek and jowl in anticipation of the festivities to follow. From my observation, ninety-percent of the crowd looked drunk, but who could really tell. I was also drunk and screaming anxiously.

To maintain crowd control, mounted police rode their horses through the crowd to thin the people out. Intermittently, they encroached on the peaceful picket line of Greyhound bus drivers who were on strike at the time. This infringement led to a heated exchange of words between the strikers and the police, and caused some confusion in the crowd control activity.

At the stroke of midnight, it seemed as if everyone fell into a state of frenzy as the ball dropped slowly to usher in the New Year. Screams, shouts, whistles and greetings filled the atmosphere as people moved about in grand jubilation. Tired and drunk, I walked away from the crowd and passed out. With the passing of the New Year, I went back to peddling my cheap articles.

One morning, for no apparent reason, a black female administrator with the Trailways bus line stopped by my vending stall to chat. First, we engaged in some small talk. Then, she asked about my reasons for being a homeless vendor in New York City. Failing to come up with a plausible answer, I told her, "I just don't know." We continued chatting for a few more minutes, and as she was about to leave she said, "Whenever you are ready to leave New York City, find me and I will give you a ticket to wherever you want to go." I thanked her and continued tending my stall. Being miserable in New York City, I felt as if God had sent another *Angel* to rescue my tortured Soul.

A few days after our conversation, I went to the lady and asked her if she could get me a ticket to Boston. "Meet me at the bus basement when you are ready and I will get you on board," she promised. Unable to control my addictive behavior, I left and came back with a six-pack of beer and some cigarettes. At the appointed time, the lady showed up, bid me goodbye and ushered me into the bus. Thanking her profusely, I watched as she turned and walked away just as the bus rolled out of the ramp. Because of her, I was on my way to Boston. Unbeknownst to both the lady and I, going to Boston would be the beginning of a new chapter in my homeless existence.

❦

CHAPTER 25
Homeless And Going To College

Traveling by bus while crisscrossing the country, I can say that I have seen God's brush strokes in two different regions, one in going into the mountains leaving Las Vegas, and another in traveling around the Chesapeake Bay going into New England. In both these regions, nature's beauty filled the atmosphere, stretching as far as the eyes could see. Captured in space and time, these places exude a sort of serenity the human senses are apt to find contagious. In some strange way, it is as if the Spiritual hand reaches out to guide the convergence of man and nature in infinite joy when traveling through these regions.

❦ ❦ ❦

The bus pulled into the Boston station snapping me out of my thoughts of God's handy works. Stepping off the bus, I went in search of a place to get a drink. This turned out to be quite easy, for not far from the bus station I saw a convenience store and went in. I bought a few beers and gulped them down. Then, I went in search of a homeless person. I learned some time ago that if I found a homeless person, and inquired from him where I could get some food, I would be directed to the homeless shelter. Luckily for me, I came upon one, then two, then several individuals who matched the descriptions of the homeless. Instead of asking for directions to a shelter, I decided to follow them since they all seemed to be headed in the same direction. As it turned out, I did not have to walk for very long. There in the midst of an industrial area, and not far from the famous Boston Globe newspaper headquarters, stood the Pine Street Inn homeless shelter.

Being in Boston felt like living life as portrayed in a history book. The names of things and places that I had studied in school came to life. I visited the replica of the ship that symbolized the famous Boston Tea Party, walked pass Crispus Atticus' grave, strolled through the Boston Commons, and stood on the campuses of Harvard, M.I.T., and the University of Massachusetts. I would later learn that education is to Boston what oranges are to Florida. Practically every community in Boston housed its own community college, and people were expected to pursue postsecondary education.

Not knowing what to do in Boston, I decided to take a visit to Boston's Main Public Library as my starting point. I became so intrigued with the books in the library, I felt compelled to make a trip there almost every day. Customarily, I quickly scanned the shelves, picked out a few books, walked over to a table in the far corner, and soon became engrossed in my reading. Especially interesting to me were the old books on philosophy and history. I read Paracelsus the German alchemist with keen interest but I am not sure how much I understood, or remembered. What I do know, I liked what I was reading. There in the library I sat, a homeless addict becoming addicted to reading books I didn't fully understand. What a homeless chutzpah?

Feeling a bit tired from reading philosophy, I decided to visit the basement of the library one day. To my surprise, the basement contained information on almost every College and University in the world. Urged on by curiosity, I inquired from the librarian on duty about the possibilities of going to college. Without much hesitation, the librarian probed my academic interests and eagerly assisted me with acquiring and filling out the necessary application and financial aid forms to Bunker Hill Community College. The anticipation and anxiety I felt at the thought of going to college lasted for several days. I prayed, I drank, I hoped, and when Bunker Hill finally accepted me as a student, I thanked God for having mercy on my homeless-alcohol-addicted Soul.

In the fall of 1991, I enrolled at Bunker Hill as Theatre Arts major. I was not prepared for what lay ahead, for I was still living in the Pine Street Inn homeless shelter. The people who operated the shelter didn't know Bunker Hill Community College accepted me as student. Afraid that they would kick me out if they found out, I literally became the homeless Jekyll and Hyde. The first part of the day I attended classes, the latter part I lived the life of a homeless bum. Probably because I was always drunk, or high on drugs, the shelter's management, as well as the other homeless residents, never suspected me of being a college student.

Living in the shelter, and going to school everyday with students who lived normal lives, felt degrading. I wondered constantly what my class mates would think of me if they found out about my homelessness. Would I be considered a traitor among them? Increasingly, I turned to drugs and alcohol to drown my humiliation and shame. The next day I showed up in class tired, hungry, and hung over. Being a student in the day and a homeless drug-addicted-drunk at night, became my daily ritual. Gradually, my humiliation began to wane, and eventually lost its negative effect. I attribute the loss to my desire to acquire a college education, and my willingness to suffer the emotional pains that came with being a homeless student.

The decision to attend college, I made on my own. I did not come from the traditional high school setting where teachers and school counselors encouraged and guided students to be college bound. I did not have any sponsors who willingly gave people like me a second chance. I was an ex-con-homeless substance-abuser, and had to face the fact and the consequences of my true identity.

To me, the path I took to college came about as a result of Divine intervention. Why I think this to be the case? The lady at the Greyhound bus terminal came to me with the offer of a bus passage to anywhere in the country. She was neither a member of my family, nor a good friend. She voluntarily offered me a ticket to go anywhere in the country. I didn't ask her for assistance. Then, I chose to go to Boston. I could have chosen any other city, in any other state, or could have gone back to Oklahoma, but I decided on Boston. Furthermore, I could have done what I did in the past, wherever I visited. That is, to go panhandling, or seeking out welfare and food stamps to stay alive and support my addictions. Instead, for whatever reason, I chose to frequent the library and inquire about attending college. These happenings made me feel that I was being guided by a higher power and that postsecondary education was part of my Spiritual Quest.

❦ ❦ ❦

Bunker Hill Community College is built on the land that once housed the former prison where Malcolm X was incarcerated in Charlestown, Massachusetts. One semester, during my studentship, Betty Shabazz, the wife of Malcolm, came to speak and accept a plaque on behalf of her deceased husband. On the same day they dedicated a statue in Malcolm's honor. I felt very proud hearing Shabaaz speak affectionately about her husband. I had never personally seen her husband, but she somehow appealed to me in the same manner her husband's oral and written works did. As she spoke of her husband's incarceration, his struggles and his quest for justice, she made me feel as if she was narrating a part of my own struggles. With her words, she painted a living picture of her husband which drew many in the audience to tears. Upon the completion of her speech, an elderly black gentleman in the audience arose from his seat, shuffled his way to the podium, handed her a bouquet of roses and kissed her on the cheek. He was in prison with Malcolm. He came, he said, to pay his regards.

❦ ❦ ❦

The requirements for some of my classes at Bunker Hill included participation in after school activities. Generally, I avoided these with some clever excuses knowing that if I arrive late at the shelter I would lose my bed. One day, I realized that many students with whom I came in contact knew of my homelessness. A few of them worked in the financial aid office, and even though I did not use the shelter as my address, they figured from my financial aid application that I had no permanent address.

Aware that a few students knew of my homeless status, I felt exposed, naked and dirty. I could no longer make excuses for not participating in their after school activities. And, knowing that I was not truthful and forthright, I wanted to run away and hide. But, where do I go? I didn't want to leave college. I enjoyed my classes, and loved the pursuit of higher education. Initially, I wanted to explain my conditions to the few students I had gotten to know, but somehow I felt they would not understand. In fact, as quickly as I thought about letting the students know of my plight, I dismissed the idea. My status in society was that of a homeless person. Being a college student did not bestow dignity on my homelessness. Upon assessing my dilemma, I came to the conclusion that I would continue my education in spite of my miserable emotional state.

Truthfully speaking, emotional upliftments for me were few and far between. One came the day the director (professor) in my Theatre Arts class offered me the role of Mr. Abernathy, the fatherly figure in *Guy's and Dolls*. It was an offer I couldn't refuse. Why? Because it would give me an opportunity to demonstrate my skills. From the day my professor gave me the script, it became a part of me. She didn't know it, but I made a silent promise to myself that I would make her proud for choosing me to be Abernathy. Religiously, I studied my lines, morning, noon, and night. I studied them during breaks between classes, while traveling on the subway; and whenever I happened to be alone, I sang out aloud as if I was performing a solo. If anyone heard me singing they probably thought I was crazy. In time, I studied my cues, my blocking and my timing, and all became a part of me.

The day came for the performance of the play. I showed up with much confidence and anticipation to go out on stage and demonstrate my acting skills. Suddenly, something struck me; I was the only black person in the play, the father figure to a young white girl, and I had to kiss her on the jaw, plus sing a solo. What if the audience finds my role intolerable? What if some people decide to walk out of the theatre in silent protest? These questions crossed my mind, but I dismissed them by imagining that I would give such a grand performance no one would notice my race. Somehow, I pulled it off, and received a standing ovation for my rendition of the song. I still am not sure whether my director gave me the part to destroy me, or show that she believed in me. However, there is one lesson she instilled in me from the first day of class; as she put it, "You have to be willing to take risks." I had taken risks all my life, and after that lesson, felt reassured about my educational pursuit.

The cast had a grand celebration after the play. I wanted to join them, but it was time for me to return to the shelter, or loose my bed.

CHAPTER 26
Met By An Angel On Bunker Hill

Traveling to and from Bunker Hill was quite easy. The college had its own subway stop which carried its name. In the center of the stop, a middle aged Irish woman named Irene established a newspaper stand. She sold Boston Globe newspapers to passers by. Rain, sleet, snow or freezing cold did not deter Irene from being at the subway stop each day to sell her newspapers. In her faint Irish accent she would call out to potential customers, "Come ova and pick up ya Globe." It seemed as if all the daily travelers knew Irene whose distinguishable trademark was her colorful head-scarves. I can't recall seeing her without one.

Irene's newspaper stand became a stopping point for many travelers and even when they don't buy her news-papers, they would hail her from a distance. It didn't take long for me to become one of Irene's regular customers. After stopping a few times to purchase the Boston Globe, I began chatting with Irene and gradually she became my best friend. She trusted me and I, her. Although she did not see very well, Irene sold her newspapers, and sorted out change with great proficiency. "Young lad, yah have to be good at whateva yah doing," she occasionally said to me. I loved the way she spoke, in a sort of melodic fashion, with one word flowing onto the other.

The friendship between Irene and I strengthened with each passing day, and so did our trust for each other. Irene trusted me to the extent that she would regularly ask me to fill-in for her at her stand while she ran errands, or went to get lottery tickets. Once, I asked her what she would do if she won the lottery; she said, "Leave it to me grands nuh."

"And what about me," I asked?

"Don't worry, I'll leave you some too," she replied rolling her rrs and lls'.

In short of money, I could always count on Irene to give me a few dollars. She knew that I drank regularly and often handed me money saying, "Heere, go have youself a pint of vodka." Irene had a sixth sense about her. She could tell when I needed something or just wanted to have a conversation with her. Almost always, she obliged.

A month before I graduated, I entrusted Irene with money for a bus ticket to Oklahoma City, Oklahoma. I had planned to join the bus immediately after the graduation ceremony, and wanted to ensure that I would have enough money for my bus fare. I also told Irene, for the first time, that I lived in the homeless shelter ever since I arrived in Boston. She just looked at me and smiled as if she already knew.

Graduation day came, and Irene and her granddaughter were there to support and congratulate me. At the end of the ceremony, I took pictures wearing my cap and gown. I also took a few pictures with Irene and her granddaughter. Afterwards, the three of us boarded the subway for the Greyhound bus station. As we stood in the crowded bus station bidding each other our final goodbyes, Irene handed me a few dollars and said, "Good luck me lad." Her parting words rang in my ears long after she and her granddaughter left. I never saw them again.

Riding the bus back to Oklahoma, I couldn't help thinking about how much I would miss Irene. She shared my moments of sadness and happiness, and listened to me in a manner no one else had done before.

As I drifted in and out of sleep on my bus ride home, I could hear Irene's voice calling out to travelers to stop by and get their newspapers. Periodically, her melodic phrases would pierce through my errant mind, reminding me that she was truly a *Guardian Angel*.

꙳

CHAPTER 27
University Education

Prior to my graduation from Bunker Hill, I attended a students' transfer-day information fair which recruiting colleges held in the lobby of the school. Personnel from various Historically Black Colleges and Universities (HBCU) attended in their hopes to recruit students who wished to transfer to four year institutions. The intent was to provide disadvantaged students with the opportunity to further their education. Among the participating institutions in the recruitment campaign was Florida A. & M. University (FAMU). Aware of FAMU's prestigious ranking among HBCU's, I inquired into transferring to this institution. As an incentive, FAMU's recruiters offered a small scholarship with admittance. The prospective student, however, must first write a letter stating his academic and professional goals. My letter to FAMU was short. I noted my poverty without disclosing my homelessness, and emphasized the pursuit of a PhD., as my ultimate goal. For some unknown reason, I enclosed a copy of Langston Hughes's poem, *Mother To Son* with my application. To this day, I still can't explain why I enclosed the poem, and am not sure whether it impacted my admission to FAMU.

❀ ❀ ❀

The members of my family congratulated me for accomplishing something worthwhile, and turning my life around when I arrived home. I didn't quite understand their fanfare. Except for the Associates Degree, I hadn't accomplished much. Materially, I achieved very little. I had no place to go, and no job offers. Financially I was broke, so how could I be considered successful. An Associates Degree by itself does not make someone successful. I guess my family never expected me to go to college and must have felt that I was destined to be a life long bum given my history of substance abuse.

Back in Oklahoma, it didn't take long for my mother and I to have a "falling out." She quit smoking, and didn't allow anyone to smoke in the house. She also criticized my drinking. This led to some disagreements. But, before the situation between my mother and I became confrontational, I moved in with my Aunt Eva. I decided things would be better if I leave until it was time for me to travel to FAMU.

I arrived on the Florida A & M University campus in the Fall of 1994. Walking up the stairs in Sampson Hall (a male dormitory) I felt as if I was climbing the stairway to heaven. I had finally made it to a University. I emptied my backpack of my few possessions and scattered them across my bed. I then went in search of a store to buy some odds and ends. Since the FAMU campus sits on the southern border of downtown Tallahassee, stores were easy to find. Walking along Adams Street which borders the east side of the FAMU campus, I found a convenience store where they sold beer, wine, cigarettes, and other everyday products. Outside of the store a group of black men stood around drinking beer. I greeted them and quickly joined their group drinking beers. In the course of our drinking, I told them that I was in Tallahassee to attend FAMU. All of them complemented me. From that first encounter the men and I became good friends. Almost everyday hence, we gathered to drink beers and "talk trash." One day the owner of the store, aware that he was in violation of the drinking ordinance, approached the group and told us not to drink beers in front of his store again. That ended our gathering.

My first day in the dorm, I sat in front of my room window drinking a beer and smoking a cigarette. Suddenly, someone shouted at me, "No one is allowed to drink or smoke in the dorm." It was the Resident Assistant (RA), and he sounded very authoritative. His demeanor made me angry. There I was, a forty seven year old man, probably the oldest resident in the dorms, and I was told that I couldn't I drink and smoke in my room? Infuriated by such ridiculous policies, I chased the resident assistant out of my room. He ran out of the door, and a short time later returned with the housing manager who asked for the key to my room. I handed him the key which he pocketed. He then took me down to the first floor of the building, opened the door to a small room that seemed like a storage closet, and gave me the key to it. "From now on this is where you will stay. If you are ever caught smoking and drinking again in the dorm, you will be thrown out."

I thought that I was being singled out unfairly until the housing manager took me into his office. As I looked around, I saw bottles of beer, wine, whiskey, knives, bongs, and other contrabands. I knew then that other students have violated dorm policies. Later, I would learn that the manager had recently implemented a new policy prohibiting the burning of incense in the rooms. The policy directly targeted students who smoked marijuana in their rooms, and used incense to guise the lingering scent of the burnt herb.

Not unlike many addicts, my relationship with dorm administrators grew increasingly hostile because I refused to heed their warnings about drinking and smoking in my room. Realizing that I was inflexible in my addictive behavior, the dorm administrator threatened me with expulsion. Each time he threatened me, I became more rebellious.

To continue my addictive lifestyle, I went in search of new means and avenues of support. It didn't take long for me to find them. On the north side of the FAMU campus ran the railroad tracks on which freight trains travel. Among a cluster of old houses behind the tracks, a group of homeless guys gathered regularly to drink and get high. I befriended the group without much difficulty, utilizing the skills I learned through my years of homelessness. It didn't take long for everyone in the group to accept me as a regular guy, and not as a college student. They seemed to care less that I attended FAMU; and if they did, they never mentioned it. Henceforth, my dual role took shape. As in my days at Boston, I became a student during the day, and an alcoholic-drug-addict at night.

One night, after an intensive use of drugs and alcohol, I passed out on the steps of Gibbs Hall, a male dormitory.

I awoke the next morning to find myself in my own bed. Apparently, the younger students, seeing my helpless body sprawled on the grass, picked me up and took me to my room unharmed. I knew they had seen me drunk in the past. Passing out at the bottom of the steps must not have surprised them at-al.

Drifting toward the homeless group seemed to have come naturally to me. They viewed me not as a stranger but as one of them. My experience with prior homelessness had taught me that the homeless did not question your intent or your motives. They do not care where you come from, or where you are going. Their concerns always focus on the present, on daily survival. The homeless with whom I associated were men who, for one reason or another, became alienated from their families, their friends, and mainstream society. These were men who grew accustomed to their broken lives. In their cycle of hopelessness, they ceased to aspire, they ceased trying to be worthy, and they ceased their search to lead normal lives. In their minds they could not be demoralized any further. I too felt the same way but only partially. I have always aspired to be successful, and saw education as my path out of the morass of poverty and homelessness. My continued association with the homeless crowd was more out of necessity, and an inner resentment of imprisonment which intensified my alienation from my family. I was a college student, but did not feel accepted as part of the college crowd. In a number of ways, I felt as a misfit among the young undergraduates.

In nineteen ninety seven, just before the end of my spring semester, I applied for and received a credit card with a seventeen hundred dollars credit limit. Afraid to let the card be posted to my university address, I had the card sent to my mother. I instructed her to forward the card to me when it arrived. With the card forthcoming, I decided that I would utilize the line of credit to set up some type of vending business as a way to earn an income. Mentally formulating my business plans, I began to envision changes in my lifestyle of drug and alcohol abuse.

The credit card arrived at my mother's address during my final exams week. For several days my mother kept calling me to activate the card. I told her I would do so when she sent it me. A few weeks after her repeated requests, my mother mailed me the card. As soon as I received the card, I called to get it activated and discovered that it was already activated. The agent with whom I spoke also informed me that eight hundred dollars worth of purchases from a pawn-shop in Oklahoma City, Oklahoma had already been made with the card. I was furious. I suspected that my mother must have used the card to get all of her jewelry out of hock. I told the credit card's agent that I didn't make the purchase and should not be held liable. After weeks of phone protests, the credit card company sent me a new card with a fresh credit line and billed my mother for the purchases on the other card.

I called my mother to tell her what had happened. In response, she informed me not to return home that summer. I was crushed. Somehow, I made it through final exams, and in spite of my mother's warnings, I decided to return home for the break. With approximately nine hundred dollars left on my new credit card, I took the bus home to Oklahoma. Getting off the bus in Oklahoma City, I decided to walk home to my mother's house. Actually, I was afraid to call anyone. Walking up the steps to my mother's house was one of the saddest moments in my life. Will she really turn me away? I asked quietly. Timidly, I knocked on the door. My mother opened it just a crack and said loud enough for me to hear, "You can't stay here, go find you a room at the mission." Never before, have I felt so rejected and scorned. My own mother turning her back on me! Without uttering a word, I turned and walked my way back to the bus station. There, I bought a ticket for the bus bounded to Tallahassee. Throughout the journey, my heavy-laden heart of emptiness never left. I cried without tears.

I could have used the credit card to get a place to stay when I arrived in Tallahassee, but I didn't. Overwhelmed with feelings of abandonment, I roamed the streets, drinking and drugging until my money ran out. A few times I stayed at the homeless shelter. Most often, however, I slept outdoors wherever I could find some comfort. Tallahassee's hot summers made crowded indoor living unbearable. To alleviate the discomfort I sought refuge outdoors sleeping on FAMU's campus, in nearby abandoned trailers, behind a building, or wherever was convenient at the time.

CHAPTER 28
Life In A Single Room Ghetto

Roaming around searching for a place to stay one day, I ran into Mona. It was as if an *Angel of God* once again showed up to rescue me. Mona helped me to get an affordable apartment down the hill from the FAMU campus. This enabled me to live in the apartment for the duration of my undergraduate years. Habitually, I drank and drugged each day after class. Routinely, I'd stop by the drug house for a small piece of crack cocaine, purchase a few of quarts of beer from the drug store, and return to my lonely apartment to pamper my addiction. I did all of this without missing my classes, and reading as much as I could. Once, in my Research Methods class, a female student sitting next to me found it difficult to withstand the lingering scent of liquor coming from me. Turning to face me she said, "You could have at least wait until the end of the day," referring to my drinking problem.

Throughout my undergraduate years at FAMU, one of the university's librarians, Mrs. Olivia Howard, reached out to help me. And, to this day she epitomizes the role of one of my *Guardian Angels*. With Mrs. Howard's assistance, I found part-time employment cleaning two auto mechanic shops near to campus. Working a few hours every day brought me enough money to buy drugs and alcohol, and a used car. A car in the hands of an addict is dangerous. Luckily for me, I didn't get into an accident. Instead, the cops arrested me for Driving Under the Influence (DUI) and suspended my driver's license. The judge sentenced me to six months probation with a stern warning to change my addictive behavior.

I cannot say for sure how Mrs. Howard must have felt knowing that I was an addict who, from time to time, found himself in trouble and yet made no effort to reform. I also do not know what she thought when I told her that I had to get rid of my car, because of a drunken driving charge. What I do know is that she found time to listen to me, and offered encouraging words as a mother to her son. I cannot recall if she ever criticized my failings. She was always patient and kind whenever I visited her. And, when I returned to FAMU to pursue the Masters degree, she again stood by me, only this time she was looking into the face of a truly reformed man, one free from drugs and alcohol.

CHAPTER 29
A Dream Gone Awry

I attended FAMU with the hope of obtaining a degree in Theatre. Ever since my days in the Oklahoma State Penitentiary, when I staged *Why Black Men Die Younger,* I became fascinated with almost all aspects of acting. I felt that participating in drama in one way or the other brings out the best in people. Even my convict acquaintances in prison felt acting gave them the opportunity to express their creativities. I still remember the many inmates who tried to befriend me when they found out that my play would be staged at the University of Oklahoma. All of them wanted a part in the play. Some hinted, and some asked outright, if they could be included in the play.

Released from prison, I never gave up on my dream to write poetry and become involved in theatre. How was I going to accomplish my goals, I never asked, I just kept focusing on my dream.

I had progressed quite well, or so I thought, towards the completion of my undergraduate degree in Theatre when everything came to a screeching halt. As a requirement for the degree, each student must cast a scene from a play to demonstrate his skills and knowledge of the theatre. Against the wishes of my director-professor, I chose a scene from Lorraine Hansbury's A *Raisin In The Sun*. The biggest problem I encountered was putting together an acting cast for the scene I had chosen. Several attempts to enlist students for my project failed. I was running out of time. Student after student politely denied my request to participate, saying that time did not permit them to learn their lines and be ready for rehearsals. Days went by without much success. I knew I was going to flunk the course and, if I did, it would delay my graduation. Contemplating what to do, a student suggested that I drop the entire semester and change my major. With no other solution at hand, I dropped the semester and changed my major to Sociology.

Selecting Sociology as my new major brought me into contact with many interesting students, and a number of dedicated professors. Since the department is housed with that of Criminal Justice, students of varied backgrounds and interests flocked the main office and hallways each day. There they discussed their interests and issues of the day. It did not take long for me join the daily gathering of students, which often took place in the company of a professor or two. Through these gatherings, I became acquainted with Professor Hunt. A slender man of my age, Mr. Hunt seemed to be the favorite among students. A consummate teacher, Mr. Hunt was sought after by students with personal or academic problems. He listened to them with much earnestness and tried to help in whatever way he could. I became one of the regulars at Mr. Hunts' office, and often joined him in the front of the Perry-Paige building where he regularly took cigarette breaks. There we talked about life during the sixties and seventies, politics of today, and most of all, our love for jazz. Mr. Hunt is an accomplished bongo drummer and loves jazz passionately.

The comradery within the Sociology and Criminal Justice department helped me to overcome my depression which resulted from having to relinquish my studies in Theatre. Learning the importance of social relationships, I reconnected with my mother and called her from time to time. I also tried to keep in contact with my ex-wife to learn of my daughter's progress. Even in my most difficult periods, the thoughts of my daughter remained alive within my very existence. In some strange way, studying sociology brought her closer to me. She resided in my thoughts, my imagination, and conscience, even though I was not there to see her take her first steps, to hug her and reassure her of my love.

Still drinking and drugging, I completed the requirements for the Sociology degree in the Fall of 1999. Finally, I can tell the world that I am a college graduate, but in some ways I was a bum with a Bachelor's degree.

Graduation ceremonies was scheduled to be held outdoors at the university's Bragg Football Stadium; Dr. William Satcher, then the Surgeon General of The United States, was invited to be the main convocation speaker. I can't recall anything the good doctor said. Suffering from a hang-over, I sat uncomfortably among the jubilant degree candidates. Under the increasingly blazing sun, I prayed for the ceremony to be over, but Dr. Satcher's speech grew longer. Adding to my misery was the list of people receiving accolades from the university. It seemed as though every Black person in Tallahassee got an award for something or the other, from honorary doctorates to meritorious awards.

Finally, the procession started. After a long list of names, mine was announced. Giddily, I stood up, walked across the stage, received a handshake from Dr. Humphries, and reached out to accept my degree in Sociology. "This is it. It's over," I mumbled as I walked off the stage.

After graduation, I remained in Tallahassee and tried to find employment. Everywhere I turned, I faced rejection. Some potential employers made polite excuses while a few openly stated that with my criminal history, I would be extremely lucky if someone hired me. Repeated rejections forced me to reassess my convictions about the rights of a born and bred American. All my life I was told that education was the way to success. No one mentioned that past imprisonment denies someone the right to gainful employment for which he is qualified. Neither FAMU nor anyone else explained this to me. After several rejections, I started thinking of the many rich men who embezzled banks and corporations, and spent time in prison only to return to more luxurious lives once released from prison. I started thinking of the men of Watergate and the Iran Contra scandal who became heroes for committing crimes against the entire nation. Overnight, they became experts, and consultants, and there I stood, scorned and ostracized, unable to find a minimum wage job. "Is this liberty and justice for all?" I asked, but no one was around to hear.

CHAPTER 30
Degreed And Out Of Luck

Unable to find employment in Tallahassee, I became quite miserable. I felt like a graduate with useless credentials. As the days passed, I fell behind in my rent, gas, light and water. City workers turned them all off because I couldn't pay my bills. For a month, I lived in utter darkness with no one to turn to for assistance. Alone, and growing depressed with each passing day, I decided to return to Oklahoma.

Some may say that I was in and out of homelessness, why not take to the streets again. The more I thought about returning to the streets, the more despondent I became. It seemed easy to be in the streets before I obtained the Bachelors degree. Working towards the degree changed my world view and my expectations. I felt I deserved a chance to earn a living, and that I have paid my dues to society. Except for me, no employer seemed to share this view. Without gainful employment, it would not take long for the street to come calling again.

In early 2000, with the aid of local black preacher, I was fortunate to get to Oklahoma City, Oklahoma. My mother and I had settled our differences pertaining to the credit card. She agreed to let me return home. Ms. Simmonds, the administrative assistant for the Sociology and Criminal Justice department at Florida A. & M., at the time, took me to the Greyhound bus station. Again, the road trip turned out to be long and arduous. I had a lot of time to think about my situation, but came up with no solutions.

Physically exhausted from the long bus ride, I was anxious to get home and take a long rest. Residing with my mother, weeks passed and I still did not have a job. To support myself, I reluctantly sought work through a day-labor employment agency. It wasn't the kind of work I expected with my college degree, but I had no alternative. Being employed felt good; I hadn't worked on a steady basis in a long time. Unfortunately for me, my mother decided to move to California to be closer to my older sister. This meant that I would no longer have a place to stay. Shortly after my mother announced her move, I focused on saving enough money to get an apartment.

Against my family's wishes, I moved into a five-unit apartment complex owned by one of my cousins. The place was a known drug haven, but I needed a place to live, and drugs and alcohol weren't new to me. I resisted using drugs for about a week. Thereafter, I was back on drugs and alcohol in full force. It got to the point where I had crack-pipes hidden all over my room. If someone came into my apartment, they would be greeted by empty wine bottles in every corner. People came to my apartment just to do drugs. I didn't have a regular job, but somehow I managed to pay the rent with assistance from my church or money from odd jobs that I performed for church members. Once more, I was on my way down on a fast moving spiral. I did drugs and alcohol because I wanted to. In the back of my mind I thought it would allow me to exist until failure had run its course. Then, I would sober up and make something of myself. As before, I lost control to drugs and alcohol. Initially, I didn't view drugs and alcohol as impediments in my quest to better myself. I attended college and saw my diploma as a valid criterion for gainful employment. Yet, every effort to find a permanent job failed. By all indications my education seemed hollow, worthless, and of no utilitarian value.

Once again, I lagged in paying my rent. I reasoned that since my cousin was the landlord, he would surely give me a break. I was wrong. When my sister called to make arrangements to pay him, he told her that he didn't want the rent money; he wanted me out of his property. I left the apartment, and after walking the streets all night, called my sister. She came and got me. I cried when she drove up. I felt distraught and defeated. There was no fight left in me. I felt I had come to the end of my road.

My sister took me to her home, and allowed me to lick my wounds for a couple of days. I thanked God for having mercy on me. One day, after some discussion about my future, my sister and I decided that I needed to check into a drug-rehabilitation program.

CHAPTER 31
Drug Rehabilitation

Spending time with my sister, I realized, through murky lenses, that I had to tread the road less traveled. We sought out a drug treatment center in Norman, Oklahoma. When I arrived at the center the lady administrator told me that they might have a vacant bed. She then asked her staff to verify the vacancy while she conducted my interview. The lady began by asking several questions ranging from how much alcohol and drugs I had taken throughout my life; to when did I start; the types of drugs and alcohol I had abused; and whether my mother, and father were alcoholics? I answered, "Yes," to the last question without providing definitive answers to the first ones. Maybe the administrator did not consider my situation critical for admission into drug rehabilitation, my mind seemed to say. In an instant, I figured that I had to find plausible explanations and fast. I decided to tell the truth, and hoped she would not deny me treatment. One by one, I rattled off the names of the drugs, and alcohol that I had taken throughout the years. When I was finished she said, "Yeah, ok, is that all?" I said "yeah," and sank back into the chair thinking I had blown my chance to be admitted for treatment. I had nowhere else to go. If I didn't get into this rehabilitation program, I would be doomed. I have never experienced such relief in my life as when the attendant came back and told the administrator that there was an open bed. After the interview, the attendant escorted me to the available bed and allowed me to say goodbye to my sister.

Bidding goodbye to my sister was very difficult. She stood by me during many of my ordeals, and there she was again helping me to find a solution to my addiction. When she left the center, I felt alone and deserted. If I am successful in my rehabilitation it would be in part to my sister's support and encouragement, I acknowledged to myself.

Sitting on the edge of the bed I couldn't help thinking how much I must have disappointed her. She credited me for completing my degree, and hinted at my need to reform. In so many ways she hoped that I would shed my addiction and find some stability in life. I was no longer a sixteen year old high school dropout or aimless drifter. I was, after all, a fifty two year old man with a college education. My addiction could no longer be blamed on youthful ignorance. The pain on my sister's face when she left me that day told me I had to succeed, I must complete the treatment.

My drug rehabilitation treatment started with a series of films, lectures, and group encounters. After looking at several films, and listening to many addicts brag about the amount of drugs and alcohol they consumed, I came to the conclusion that drug rehab was the sort of process through which you got clean, go back to abusing drugs and alcohol, and then return for additional treatment. As an increasing number of addicts involved in the group encounters told their stories, they helped to reaffirm my impression that addiction was an endless cycle of abuses leading into oblivion.

After receiving months of treatment, several people left the program and came back because they relapsed. As each left and returned, the stories of their continued addiction changed with each group encounter. In sum, nearly all of the stories they told bordered on some sort of victimization in which they were the underdogs. As I listened to their tall tales, I would shake my head in quiet disbelief. There I sat in the company of con-artists, each trying to out-con other con-artists, all in the name of reform.

Going to Alcoholics Anonymous was mandatory. I didn't mind attending the meetings, but what I found bothersome was the treatment center's silent policy on giving lip service to "making progress." I couldn't do it; I was not making any progress and felt so deep inside of me. Other than providing me a place to lay my head for a while, the center had not done much to rehabilitate me; I still felt like an alcoholic and a drug addict. Furthermore, given the chance, I felt I would revert back to addiction, since the program did not prepare me for anything else. After six-months at the treatment center, the administrator threw me out for being one of the unsuccessful cases.

Momentarily, my attitude worsened. Inwardly, I hated everything. Ever since my wrongful arrest I grew bitter by leaps and bounds, but lacked the power or wherewithal to stop my decline and degradation. Suddenly a few thoughts struck, *I have not had a drink or used any drugs in about six months. I did so, not because of any treatment, but because I detested the hypocrisy in the so called rehabilitative efforts which proved to be nothing more than the recycling of addicts.* Then a corollary thought unfolded: *If certain forces in the society operate to destroy people like me, then it is me who must find ways to combat them.* With these thoughts in mind, I knew I benefited from my stay at the treatment center because it allowed me time for introspection.

CHAPTER 32
On The Road Again: New Orleans and Mississippi

Expelled from the center, I called my sister to let her know that I was on my way over to her house. She was furious, and immediately said, "You can't stay here Junior." Disappointed, I didn't say anything else and simply hung up the phone. I couldn't assure my sister of my determination to self reform, especially since I failed in the past. After allowing me to spend a night at her house, she drove me to the treatment center the next day to collect the money I left there. Except for a few words now and again, my sister remained silent throughout the drive. I could sense her unhappiness with me, but fear kept me from saying anything, or to even apologize. Retrieving my money from the center, my sister then drove me to the bus station. "Take care Junior," she said as she drove off.

By now, it seemed as though I had spent half of my life in buses traveling to wherever my few dollars would take me.

I must have stood at the ticket counter some twenty minutes trying to decide where to go. I had two hundred dollars saved while at the treatment center, and now I wanted to put Oklahoma behind me. I asked the ticket agent to give me some suggestions on where to go, "What about New Orleans?" the man promptly said. I told him that I had never been to New Orleans, and decided to flip a coin where heads meant New Orleans, and tails, Miami. Tossing the coin it landed on its head. I then bought a ticket to New Orleans, Louisiana.

The Mississippi River runs through downtown New Orleans in the shape of a crescent, from which the name Crescent city originated. I can't quite explain why, but my soul came alive in New Orleans. I walked the streets for a while observing the people and the buildings. The excited shoppers, the party goers, the hustlers and the passersby, all converge in what seemed to me like one unending gala. The festive atmosphere felt truly contagious, and for a while I forgot that I had no place to go. Snapped out of my dream like state by the shrill sirens of a police car, I walked a few city blocks looking for nothing in particular. In less than two days, I became acquainted with some of the homeless guys who hustled along Canal Street and the French Quarter. Knowing them made my transition to the city much easier. For a short time, I hung out with the homeless during the daytime, engaging in small talk and testing my will to resist drugs and alcohol. At nights, I looked for any hole to lay my head for a few hours.

My familiarity with the City of New Orleans grew with each passing day. To start my day, I would go down to the Mississippi River behind Canal Street, and pray. I can't remember when it started, but I had made it a practice to pray each day, thanking God for protecting me throughout my tumultuous years of drinking, drugging and living in the streets. My daily praying signaled the beginning of profound changes within me. I didn't realize it at the time since my transformation unfolded gradually. It seemed that in the absence of Guardian Angels, my heart and soul slowly opened up to the silent voice of the Lord.

One day, I went into the Voo Do museum, and while signing the visitor's book met an old black lady with braided hair. "Can I help you Sir?" she asked. "You have been calling me all my life and now I am finally here," I answered. Awe-struck by my response, the old lady stared at me for a while as if trying to make sense of what I had said. I too was unsure why I responded to her question in the manner I did. It was as if something had wrested control from me, and forced me to acknowledge her presence in this strange fashion. Maybe the Lord wanted me to meet this old lady, and therefore directed our encounter, I reasoned. I left the museum with the lady still staring occasionally in my direction. I never saw her again.

As faith would have it, there are some things in life I couldn't seem to escape; being detained by the police comes to the fore. One night, while sleeping under the Canal Street Bridge, the police arrested me for violating city ordinances. I spent ten days in jail. Upon my release, I decided to get into a program at the Oz (Ozanon Inn, a homeless shelter on Camp Street in New Orleans). The Oz, considered the premiere center for the homeless in New Orleans, offered breakfast and lunch seven days a week. It also provided a bed to sleep in nightly, and made available a host of other services to homeless males in the city. Spending a couple of days there made me realize that I needed to move on; but to where, I did not know.

Residing at the Oz, I had to get up at five o' clock every morning to help set up the dinning room for breakfast. Afterwards, I washed the dishes and cleaned the dish room. These duties remained the same for lunch. In the evenings, I served sandwiches to men who came in to spend the night. My existence at the Oz turned out to be a lesson in perseverance, humility, and faith. Finding it difficult to adjust to the regimented lifestyle, I drifted into a state of laxity, and after six-months, left the program.

Through a series of transactions, I hustled enough money to get to Shreveport, Louisiana. There, I spent a few nights on the streets. I then went and enrolled in a detox center, not because I started abusing drugs and alcohol again, but because I needed a safe place to stay. Later, I managed to get into the drug rehabilitation program at the Buckhalter. Buckhalter turned out to be the best program I have ever entered. It enabled me to actually continue my introspection, and listen to the Divine messages entering my Soul.

Housed in an old hotel in downtown Shreveport, the program had separate rooms for every male and female. Addicts at Buckhalter participated in daily group activities which served to unite them as one big extended family. Everyone attended Alcoholics Anonymous seven days a week, and received group therapy five days a week. Since I no longer abused alcohol, I went through the counseling process as a form of reaffirmation.

The counselors at Buckhalter went about their work conscientiously as if the rehabilitation of addicted clients truly mattered. On my first interview, my assigned counselor asked somewhat bluntly, "What is it that you are looking for in life?" I lifted my head, looked straight into his eyes and responded, "Someone to believe in me." He paused for a moment with a surprised look on his face. Then, leaning forward on his desk, he asked a few more questions, jotted down some notes, and left.

The bluntness with which the counselor asked his questions impacted me minimally. Scrutinized and queried in every which way by police officers, drug counselors, judges, university administrators, parents, brothers and sisters, had enabled me to become less sensitive to such frankness. Bluntness aside, the Buckhalter counselor did show genuine concern for me - his client. He did not approach me with indifference or make me feel hopeless. In fact, he left me feeling worthy.

At Buckhalter, three major violations could get you kicked out of the program: having sex with one of the females, smoking cigarettes - you had to sign an agreement to quit smoking cigarettes to get into the program - and relapsing - using drugs or alcohol - while in the program. I experienced the same problem in this program as I did with other programs. That is, I found it difficult to suppress my prolonged feelings of mistrust for others. In addition, my conviction that people would manipulate you for their own benefits and then discard you still held sway. Harboring such attitudes and beliefs, however, continued to serve to my detriment.

Spending almost six months at Buckhalter, and showing very little change in attitudes and behaviors, administrators decided to release me from their program. It appeared that this length of stay had become my residential norm to drug rehab. Once again, released for failure to cooperate, I hustled a few dollars for a bus ticket out of Shreveport. I went to the bus station in Shreveport with forty-dollars in my pocket; I asked the ticket agent how far out of Louisiana can I go on forty-dollars? She told me that I could get as far as Vicksburg, Mississippi. I then bought a ticket to Vicksburg without knowing its location, or what I would find there.

The bus arrived in Vicksburg, Mississippi to find the station closed. I disembarked, took a quick look around, and started walking as if I knew my destination. The sun had already set. Darkness filled the air. Adding injury to insult, the bus station stood on the outskirts of town, a good distance from everything else. Without any means of transportation, I took to the highway on foot, traveling in the direction I thought might take me to downtown.

Strolling down the road, I felt as if I had stepped out into the unknown, and was once again on a spiritual journey. Ever since leaving my sister's home, feelings of spirituality entered and fled my mind with greater frequency. Increasingly, I began to take notice. Was God sending me messages? I asked as I walked on to nowhere in particular. If God was sending me messages, why aren't they clear? I paused for a moment searching for answers, and when none came, I pushed the thoughts out of my mind.

⁂

Some years later, while enrolled in graduate school, I had a discussion about my experiences with one of my professors. Although we uphold different faiths, I would engage him in discussions about my beliefs. One morning, after a restless night, I asked:

"Doc, do you believe that God sometimes try to talk to you?"

Looking quizzically at me he said: "I believe so. But, why do you ask?"

"Well, sometimes I get these strange feelings as if someone is trying to tell me something. As a matter of fact, it started a few years ago, back in Oklahoma," I explained.

"When you say strange, what do you mean?"

"I don't know if I can explain it. I usually feel a change in me. I feel as if my body gets lighter, and I am guided by someone."

"Guided, like someone has tapped into your mind and taken over your feelings and actions?"

"Yeah, something like that."

"You haven't started drinking or using drugs again, have you?" he probed

"Come on Doc, you know I haven't had a sip of beer or any illegal drugs in years," I responded.

"Well Ulyses, I believe that within all of us there is a Spirit Being, and it is *that* part of us that can communicate with God."

"But how do you know?"

"I don't. I am going solely on my belief."

"Come…on now, tell me what you think," I insisted.

"I think that you first have to discover that Spirit Being within you. I try to do it though meditation."

"Have you ever gotten any messages?"

"I believe so."

"How have you used these messages?"

"To be honest with you, I am aware of it only occasionally. Sometimes when some one says something, or something occurs, it makes me realize retrospectively that I did sense it, but brushed it aside."

"I am not clear on it, can you explain some more?" I asked.

"God has equipped us with a curious mind. Think of how fast the mind works and the thousands, maybe millions of thoughts that run through it each day. Can we focus on, or remember them all?"

"No I guess we can't."

"Contained in those thousands, or millions of microscopic thoughts that runs through our minds each day are messages from God, but we don't realize or acknowledge them because we are so preoccupied with our material existence which dominates the receptacles in our consciousness."

"You lost me."

"Let me put it this way. We are so focused on our material well being, we seldom think of anything else. We clutter our minds with finding ways to improve our material circumstance, more so than our spiritual well being. The materially cluttered mind is seldom alert to spiritual pricks, much less spiritual conversations."

"But what about me, I was bent on self-destruction rather than material comfort."

"I am not saying that I know or have an answer. It could be that you were preoccupied with your pain and suffering which forced you to contemplate, even momentarily, on your fate. In so doing, you may have relaxed the mental barriers that blocked the spiritual message flowing through you."

"I am not sure about all of this. What I do know is that I felt an awakening within me, in which an unseen force gently guided me on my reformed addict's course."

CHAPTER 33
From the Rescue Mission to Graduate School

Walking along the highway, I came upon a guy whom I asked directions to the nearest mission where I could get a night's rest. "There isn't any mission downtown," he said, and directed me the Rescue Mission on Washington Street. "They might accept you there," he hollered at me while walking away. Thanking him, I continued on, still unsure about my destination.

I must have walked for over a mile when I happened to see a lady. I asked her for directions to the Rescue Mission. "Keep on going straight and you will find it," she said with a short pause, and then added, "It is already closed, but if you knock on the door they will let you in."

When I reached the mission, I did not see any lights coming from the inside. The doors were also closed. Using my fist, I pounded on the door a few times pausing between three or four rapid knocks. Someone opened the door. Once inside, two of the guys who let me in told me that I was lucky to get in at that time of night. After talking to me about the program, they signed me up.

I had never traveled to this part of the South before. Truly, it was an edifying experience. The residual effects of slavery seemed to be present everywhere I turned. The servility of the Black residents could be seen and felt in all corners of the town. White folks maintained their social distances even though they interacted with Blacks daily. I did not see any of them partaking in any form of inter-racial fraternizing.

The Rescue Mission where I stayed operated a mandatory religious program. All residents had to attend church twice daily. New residents spent their first ninety days working in the warehouse, loading, unloading and sorting donations for sale in the thrift store. Upon completion of the ninety days warehouse labor, residents were transferred into an adjoining house for ninety-days. Assisted in finding jobs, house residents paid rent, and worked their way back into the mainstream society. For some unknown reason, my attitude changed while I was in the program. It appeared as if a sense of order came into my life, one that I had never experienced before.

During my stay at the Rescue Mission, we visited a few small Black churches in the back woods of the county. Black people in Mississippi seemed to be closer to God than any people that I have met. When they prayed, you felt their sincerity in seeking mercy, and when they sang they touched your Soul with glory. Listening to, and watching these poor Black folks appeal to God shook me with moments of enlightenment.

Completing my ninety days work in the warehouse, I moved into the adjoining house, and from there got a job as a dishwasher at the Walnut Hills restaurant. The fact that I had a Bachelor's Degree in Sociology did not elevate my status any, for I was the lowest man on the totem pole at Walnut Hills. The other Black employees loved it, and in some ways derived pleasure in having an educated Black man working for less than they.

From the inception, dishwashing proved to be a humiliating experience, but I endured. Upon the completion of my ninety days stay at the adjoining house, I rented a small room at a cheap motel downtown. There, in my own quiet surroundings, I regularly evaluated my past and thanked God for bringing me thus far. It was He who sent the human angels who helped to keep me alive throughout my homeless wanderings.

Renting a small room of my own, and working for wages aided me in becoming independent. Since I gave up drinking and drugging, I worked towards bringing greater stability into my life. I bought a used car to travel around town. One day, while driving through an intersection, another car failed to yield the right of way, hit me and totaled my car. The police did not charge the young female driver even though she caused the accident and drove an uninsured car. A few weeks later Refusing to repair my car, my insurance company reimbursed me the premium I had paid.

In Vicksburg, my dependency on drugs and alcohol drifted further and further away with the passing of each day. Over time, I felt whole and comforted. I read the Bible at every opportunity, and prayed to God for strength to stay the course of my healing. Spiritually, I felt increasingly awakened. As my healing progressed, I began to think more about my future.

With a small savings from my meager income, I decided to call Florida A. & M. University to see how much it would cost to clear up my debt, and have my undergraduate diploma sent to me. Informed by the registrar's office that it would only cost me nine dollars to have my diploma mailed, I rushed to the post office, purchased a money order and sent it out to the university. When my diploma arrived, I felt a sudden rebirth. I kissed it, and after having it framed put it away safely.

The receipt of my diploma renewed my hunger for higher education. What if I could return to college to pursue graduate studies? Even if I wanted to do so, how would I pay for my education? My income was quite small, and I had only a few dollars saved. Maybe I am dreaming, or maybe I am losing my sanity, I struggled with these thoughts. Questions after questions, thoughts after thoughts poured into my mind. To quell the mental anguish, I called Florida A. & M. University, convinced that I should apply for graduate school, and pursue a master's degree. Within a week, I received the requested graduate admission forms, filled them out and a few weeks later received conformation of acceptance into the Masters in Applied Social Sciences Program.

Elated at the opportunity to pursue graduate studies, I told the owner of the restaurant that I would be going back to school the first of the year. She didn't seem pleased. I brushed her displeasure aside and proceeded with my plans to attend graduate school. The fact that I didn't have any money to pay for anything, or a place to live did not deter me from returning to FAMU. In December of 2002, I left Vicksburg, Mississippi with my backpack of my few necessities, and headed to Tallahassee. I cannot honestly explain how it all happened, except to say that the Divine once again must have intervened on my behalf.

CHAPTER 34
Homeless In Pursuit Of A Masters Degree

How does a homeless person become a graduate student? I didn't have answers, just the will to learn. I did what I felt anyone pursuing a dream would have done. At the end of December 2002, I arrived in Tallahassee, again with no money, and no place to live. My only possessions were my backpack, and my acceptance letter to graduate school. The first few days I hung out at my old haunts, and spent a couple of nights with some people I knew from my days as an undergraduate. Before the start of the Spring semester, I contacted the graduate office and enrolled for classes. Graduate school officials told me not to stop attending classes even though I couldn't pay tuition. Their decision gave me hope that I would be able to secure some type of financial assistance to work toward the Masters degree. Next, I had to find a place to stay.

Finding a place to stay proved more difficult than enrolling for classes. With no money, I gave up on renting my own room. Fully aware that I couldn't continue to live on the streets and attend classes, I sought refuge at the homeless shelter. Located on Tennessee Street across from the city's bus depot, and about a mile from the FAMU campus, the shelter is easily accessible by bus. Penniless and jobless, I couldn't have selected a better place to stay, at least for a short while. During my intake at the shelter, I made it clear that I intended to attend graduate school. Everyone present seemed apprehensive about my declaration. I felt as if they wanted to ask, "How can a homeless person go to college for a Masters degree? And, if he already has a bachelors why doesn't he find a job?" The snickers on their faces gave away their doubts about my decision.

Customarily, at the Tallahassee homeless shelter, if you slept on the floor for ten straight days you became eligible for a bed. I did my ten days on the floor and then the director gave me a bed. After explaining to him that my classes ended after the shelter's closing time, he agreed to relax the rules to accommodate my late arrival.

Leaving the shelter early in the mornings and arriving late in the afternoons, I hardly had time to shower. For a while I went without a bath or a change of clothes, and showed up for classes dirty and smelling bad. What my classmates thought of me I do not know. None openly expressed discomforts, or said anything to the professors about my physical disposition. I am not sure whether they knew I was sleeping at the shelter while taking classes. If any of them suspected, they never asked me any questions. Why am I mentioning this now? It is testimony to some of the things I had to undergo to fulfill my dream of acquiring my education.

Entering my professor's office one morning he asked, "Did you see the early morning news?"

"No. Why do you ask?"

"Are you sure you didn't see the early morning news?" he asked as if to make certain that I was telling him the truth.

"Come on Doc, is this a joke or something? You know I live in the shelter and I don't have a television."

"Well, there was a story about a student who slept a few nights in his university's library. They said he was homeless."

"You mean they call someone sleeping in the library for a few nights homeless?"

"Apparently so."

I thought for a moment then asked, "Was he white or black?"

"White," he said with a grin.

"What do you think Doc, if they had caught me sleeping in the library for a few nights?"

"Call the cops and have you thrown in jail of course," he replied.

I laughed so hard I couldn't control myself. It seemed my professor read my thoughts.

I rushed out of my professor's office and went in search of a national newspaper. Finding one, I hurriedly opened it and searched for the story. Suddenly, there on one of the pages, I saw a picture of the student along with his story about sleeping in his university's library. In reading the article, I began to think of how the media covers colored and non-colored people differently. Reading the article more than once, I became convinced that the young white student did not know the true meaning of homelessness. Among the homeless he would be considered a homeless fraud. Maybe my professor is right. If it was me, school officials would most definitely have called the cops instead of the media.

Back at the shelter each day, I kept to myself. I read a lot and took notes. Sometimes, a drunk or two would get into an argument with each other, but I learned not to pay any attention. Overall, the shelter was fairly quiet since most residents kept to themselves. Most of the talking came from the staff and volunteers engaged in quiet discussions, answering questions or giving orders.

Even though I slept at the shelter every night, I decided not to eat and hang around there more than necessary. How I arrived at this decision I am not sure except to say that I felt I had little in common with the other homeless folks. To the outsider, this statement might sound funny because of my own status as a homeless person. It was true that I had no home, or income to rent an apartment, and slept at the shelter. However, my daily activities and goals were different from the other homeless residents. I aspired to have a doctorate degree one day. If, in the pursuit of it, I have to suffer homelessness, then so be it. Maybe there are other homeless individuals like me, but I have not met any of them. In fact, I have not even heard of them.

Not eating meals provided by the shelter left me on the brink of starvation almost daily. I ate only what I could garner, and what I received from my friends, a few of whom worked at the university's library. My most difficult times with hunger happened to be on the week-ends and holidays. With fewer people working at the university during these periods, and with most of the buildings closed, I would spend time reading in the library and walking leisurely around the campus until it was time to return to the shelter to sleep. If I happened to see someone I knew, I asked for a few dollars to buy a meal or two. Otherwise, I would return to the shelter hungry, and hope that my luck would improve the next day.

Several months after enrolling in my first graduate class, I received a Graduate Assistantship from the university. Filled with happiness, I thanked the Lord for intervening once again on my behalf – for delivering me from despair. I am not sure how it happens, but it seems that whenever I am on the brink of calamity a guiding hand reaches out to someone to come to my aid.

Ever since arriving on FAMU's campus, I kept in touch regularly with the various administrative offices inquiring about financial assistance. In just a couple of months, I must have received over a hundred excuses, and sent to practically every office on campus, each time receiving the same feedback, "We don't have anything at the moment but you can try again later... Have you tried ...such and such... office? ... Why don't you try ...such and such... office?" The multitude of rejections served to strengthen my resolve instead of breaking my will. I kept up my inquiry for assistance. And, when no one seemed willing to take a chance on me, Ms. Dedra Azonabi stepped forth.

At the time, Ms. Azonabi served as the director of the *Life Gets Better & Thur*good *Marshall* Scholarship Program. Showing up at her office, most often unannounced, Ms. Azonabi found time to listen to me and offer some encouraging words, "You must not give up Ulyses, something will work out," she would say. I am not sure if Ms. Azanobi realized how much her words helped me to keep on hoping. And, just about the time I thought nothing good would ever come my way, Ms. Azonabi one day recommended that I talk to Dr. Chanta M. Haywood, the Dean of Graduate Studies. I left Ms. Azanobi's office that day with mixed feelings. "Is this another form of rejection? Is this Ms. Azinobi's way of getting rid of me?" one part of me questioned while the other half responded, "This may be my chance. Ms. Azinobi has always been honest with me."

I must have sat in Dr. Haywood's outer office for about ten minutes but it felt like almost an hour. With each passing minute my hopes lifted and faded. To pass the time, I tried to read, but my mind roamed around in a sort of derangement, "What if I am rejected? What would I do?" From the inner doorway of the office a lady approached. Extending her hand she said, "Hi I am Dr. Haywood; you must be Ulyses,"- both of us saying Ulyses at the same time. Meeting Dr. Haywood for the first time brought me face to face with one of my many *Guardian Angels*. She listened to my plight, and took mercy on my impoverished soul, granting me a full fellowship to complete the Masters of Applied Social Science degree.

Throughout my conversation with Dr. Haywood, I found myself clutching to her every word. Her soft spoken voice dispelled my discomforts, and her bright smile made me feel that she cared about my education. Putting on my best plea, I told her about some of my life struggles, and my inward hunger for an education up to the doctoral level. She listened with keen interest and at the end of our conversation, offered me a Graduate Assistantship. Before leaving her office she challenged me to do well and assured me that her door was always open if I ever needed to see her.

"FAMU's students should be thankful to have someone like Dr. Haywood," I mused as I left her office and walked across campus to inform my Criminal Justice professors of my success. Dr. Haywood truly cares and would prove it time and again during the period of my studentship. I remember calling her several times at short notices asking her if she could meet with me, and each she reminded me, "My door is always open Ulyses." In the wilderness of my troubled homeless life, the dean's reassurance of her open door kept alit my burning desire for graduate education.

CHAPTER 35
My Campus Family

Pursuing the Master's degree enabled me to make new friends, rekindle old relationships, and establish more enduring connections with all. Still homeless, but no longer an addict, I spent most of my time reading in the library, and talking to undergraduate students outside of the Benjamin Perry classroom building where I shared an office with Dr. P, one of my professors.

My decision to be Dr. P's graduate assistant created some confusion initially. It seemed that others had more questions about my choice than Dr. P himself. Without consulting him, I chose him to be my "major professor," and when I informed him of my decision, all he said, "You must be prepared to excel Ulyses." The amusing part about my choice was that some people had more concerns about my decision than me.

I chose Dr. P because I considered him, not only as a professor, but as true mentor and friend. He stood by me in my troubled addictive undergraduate years. When I returned to undertake graduate studies, he embraced me despite my continued state of homelessness. I remember one evening as I walked the hallway to my classroom on the fourth floor of the Perry-Paige building, I came upon Dr. P and Mr. Hunt. Engaged in conversation, they both looked up and saw me walking towards them. "Look who is here?' they both shouted almost in unison. "We were just talking about you," Dr. P said. "You putting me on," I said with a grin. "No, no," Mr. Hunt intervened, "We were really talking about you, wondering about where you were, and what you were doing." After letting them know that I was accepted in graduate school, I left for my class. "Stop in and see me," Dr. P said as I walked on. This encounter marked the beginning of my renewed relationship with Dr. P.

In my view, the greatest compliment a teacher can receive is when a former student comes back to him or her for guidance. This, in effect, is the measure of the teacher's true worth. I know of many professors during my undergraduate years whom I would prefer to forget. I also know several professors whom students adore, and regularly sought after. The latter is the group who made education exciting, and being a student worthwhile.

Two other people within the Criminal Justice Department who also opened up their arms and embraced me as a family member are Dr. Dix, and Ms. Perkins. Both of these women genuinely care about students and would spend countless hours encouraging and advising them. Together with Dr. Hamilton from FAMU's Psychology department, they became my campus family. At lunch we would gather together to feast on whatever was available, whether it was tuna sandwiches, or simply crackers and cheese. It was not what we ate, but the beauty of the moments we shared. We talked about any and everything, politics, sports, social events, families and most often the state of black education. Without fail, we would arrive at the same conclusions: *Young students' emphasis on material gratification instead of their education; And, the opportunities they squander will never be regained.*

Through the discussions I've had with my campus family, I was able to put my own life in perspective. Several books also helped me with my self analysis. These include: Carl Upchurch *Convicted in the Womb*; Patrice Gaines *Laughing in the Dark,* and Nathan McCall *Makes Me Wanna Holler.*

Upchurch, McCall and Gaines enabled me to dissect my troubled past. All of these writers, like me, journeyed through America's prison system. Like me, they loved to read, like me, they understood the value of a good education, but unlike me they didn't suffer the severity of homelessness. Upchurch, in particular, impressed upon me the plight of the Black child, one who is convicted from the time of conception. In many ways, I too felt I was convicted because of my blackness. McCall brought to life the problems some black men suffer even when they have a father in the home. In capturing the turbulent relationship he had with his father, he helped me to better understand some of mine. And, Gaines brought hope into my once addicted soul. She taught me how to find hope within myself. Altogether, these writers taught me to persevere. In dissecting their lives they assisted me in an anatomy of my homeless soul.

CHAPTER 36
A Different Encounter with the Police

Given my history of arrests, I never thought I would have a pleasant encounter with the police, but a series of events led to a meeting with Tallahassee's police chief which gave me a different perspective on policing. This is how it came about.

While serving as his graduate assistant, Dr. P asked that I accompany him on his field visits to monitor the activities of student-mentors in the Juvenile Justice Role Model Development Program (JJRMDP). "Ulyses,' he said one morning as soon as he arrived at the office, "I would like for you to go out with me into the community and schools to see how well our mentors are doing."

"Come on Doc, you know I can't do that," I responded.

"What happen, are you afraid?"

"No Doc, I'm not afraid. You know my history of arrests precludes me from being a mentor."

"I know that; and I am not asking that you become a mentor on a one-on-one basis. I want you to serve as a guest speaker. Lets' put it this way, you'll be a "deterrent-motivation" speaker for lack of a better term."

Still reluctant, I said, "Doc, you know I don't like to talk too much about my past, and who cares about it anyway?"

"You know Ulyses, I don't understand. You have so much to offer; how can I tell kids what its like to be arrested and detained? These things never happened to me. The problem with the current day mentoring initiative is that it screens out the people who can be more effective in turning around the lives of at risk youths; people like you who have the experience that can be shared as a form of deterrence. Most of what I have learned about delinquency and crime comes from text books, and conversations with a few convicts. You, however, have the lived experience which, when shared, would have a greater impact on the at-risk."

"I agree with you Doc, but parents would scream, teachers would scream and the public would scream. Is that what you want? Are you prepared for the attack?"

"It's not like you were a pedophile or some big time criminal, Hooks," Professor P said, addressing me by my last time. Whenever he used my last name, I knew he didn't fully agree with my viewpoint.

"I know that, and you know that Doc, but the people out there who screams the loudest truly don't want to help kids who are really in trouble. Their intent is to make money out of troubled kids, incarcerate them, and then bid to manage the facilities that house them."

"Forget the debate. Are you coming with me or not?"

"OK, I can see you are mad with me. I'm coming."

After our conversation, we drove to the low income community where JJRMDP students serve as mentors. There, we met first with the community coordinator, a very articulate and dedicated woman in her late thirties. While talking to the coordinator, a little girl ran up to the lady; taking her by the hand she asked, "Ms. A… can you take me to jail?" At first, no one paid the little girl any attention. Still holding on to the coordinator's hand she pleaded, "Ms. A…, please take me to jail, please Ms.A …, please," Bending down to hold the little girl's hand, my professor asked, "Honey, why do you want to go to jail?" Instantly she replied, "Cause, I want to see my daddy." The little girl's response touched my inner conscience, and brought me an instant jolt of pain. She knew that jail kept her daddy away from her, but did she have any concept of jail? None, I'm sure.

Later we met with the housing manager to talk about the effects of the mentoring efforts, and the social problems that plague the community. He asked if we could arrange for a meeting with the Tallahassee police chief to discuss delinquency and crime in the community, and what could be done to address the problem. Dr. P arranged the meeting and asked that I attend. "Doc," I said, "you know my relationship with the police and none of it was pleasant. Why would I want to go with you?"

"How many little girls like the one you saw, have lost their fathers to the prison system? Take a guess. Like you, some of the fathers are probability innocent. How many times have you sat across from the police without being questioned about a crime or being under arrest?"

"None, as far as I can recall," I said in answer to his last question.

With notepad in hand, the housing manager, my professor and I entered the police station. "We are here to see the Chief," my professor explained. An officer escorted us upstairs to the Chief's office after we signed the visitors' log. The Chief, a tall lean and stately African American gentleman, stood up and greeted us with outstretched hands. The manner in which the Chief welcomed us erased some of the residual trepidation I had for the police. He discussed crime and delinquency in the community with such sincerity, I wondered what my life would have been had I met someone like him before. I probably would not have had such bitter experiences with police officers.

For a greater part of my life, I felt victimized by the police and the justice system. And, there across from me, sat a concerned police chief talking about the problems of youths with deep sensitiveness about their future. Scribbling on my notepad as fast as I could, I tried to capture every word uttered by the Chief. He lamented the arrests of seven and eight year old grade school children. He talked about teenagers and their problems. He talked about college graduates and their arrests records, and then he said, "I hurt for their future."

The Chief's last remarks touched me deeply. I felt as if he spoke directly to me. There, before him I stood, a living example of what he meant about the future of someone with a history of arrests. I have had more job rejections than I could count, laughed at for doing menial work while holding a college degree, stigmatized and rejected for serving time in prison and residing in homeless shelters. And, last but not least, I couldn't even volunteer my services for free, serving as a mentor to an at-risk youth. In my view, the Chief summed up my personal problems eloquently.

Driving back to campus with my professor that day, I laughed to myself.

"What made you so happy?" Dr. P asked.

"What do you mean?"

"Don't answer my question with a question. You've been laughing as if you hit the jackpot or something."

"I was just laughing because I find it odd sitting with cops, and I was doing some of the questioning. I never dreamt that such a thing would ever be possible for me. I was the one always being questioned by cops, not the one questioning cops. Strange is the life of a homeless ex-con."

CHAPTER 37
Going to Prison But Not as an Inmate

If someone had said to me that I would be going to prison without being arrested, I would have laughed in his face. Little did I realize that such a visit would one day be possible! After spending a better part of my youth behind prison walls, I swore I would never see the inside of a prison again. The likelihood therefore, that I would be behind prison walls again seemed remote. I was wrong.

In the Spring of 2003, I enrolled in a course on Correctional Management. The adjunct instructor who taught the course held a permanent administrative position at the women's correctional facility in Tallahassee. On the first day of class, he announced that he intended to present an insider's view of prison programs, and would also arrange for the class to visit the facility. As soon as the class ended, I went up and whispered to him that I had spent several years in prison. "That is not a problem," he said. "But I live in the homeless shelter and do not have any means of transportation to go to the facility when the time comes," I whispered in reply. "Don't worry," he responded, "I will pick you up."

The day of the visit, the instructor picked me up on campus, and we rode to the facility located some eight miles away on the outskirt of town. On our way, he inquired about my incarceration and homelessness, and made offers of food and clothing which I declined.

Most of the students were already at the facility when we arrived. Looking into their faces, I could sense that they were unaware about life behind bars. Despite my years of incarceration, I had mixed feelings about the visit. First, I had never entered a prison except as an inmate. "Would it feel any different as a visitor?" I silently asked myself. "What kind of memories would the visit evoke?" Before I could answer my own questions, we were guided through a couple of large steel doors leading to the inside of the prison.

"A few years ago, this facility used to be a Federal prison for men, but today it's a women's prison," our instructor who served as our guide said as he began the tour. Stopping close by to a group of women who just stood around chatting, he said, "Many of the women you see in this facility are here for serious offenses. Some were in the drug trade and some have committed murder." When he said this, I glanced over at the group of women to see if I could detect the hardened criminals but couldn't. From their smiles and laughter, they all appeared to be having a good time looking at us looking at them.

As we continued to tour the facility, our guide pointed to a school, and explained the types of education offered. He took us next to the recreational facility and talked about sports competition among inmate teams. Thus far into the tour, I didn't have any flashbacks about my life in prison. Perhaps it was because I never participated in sports while in prison, and even though I studied for the G.E.D, and read a lot, the conditions did not look the same. The women's prison looked more like a secluded hideaway for wayward ladies.

"I want to see the real bad ladies," someone muttered, "I want to see what they look like." No sooner had the person finished the remark, we came upon an area that had fences and rows and rows of barbed wires. Our guide signaled us to stop for a moment. "Can anyone guess who are kept here, behind these gates and fences?" No one answered. The expressions on their faces indicated that they knew, especially when the inmates behind the fences started whistling and calling out to the guys. "Look at that one, he is cute," an inmate said pointing to one of the male students. "I want him," another inmate said pointing to another male student.

Walking away from the women housed in the maximum security area we could still hear their calls and sexual comments.

We stopped next at the furniture factory where the prison inmates assembled tables, desks and chairs, for sale to various state agencies. To the amazement of many in my tour group, the inmates wielded electric drills, saws and welding torches with such dexterity that brought forth comments such as, "That lady works like a man," and "I never seen a woman welder before, she got to be one tough lady."

Listening to these comments and observing the women at work, caused me to recall my own incarceration. Inmates labored in the prison factories similar to regular employees in the labor market. They earned allowances that they used to purchase cigarettes and other basic necessities such as soap, toothpaste and sometimes illegal drugs.

On our way back from the prison that day, my instructor asked me about the visit. "Very interesting," I said.

"Did you learn anything?" he asked.

"Not much. Prisons are the same everywhere?"

"You really think so?"

"Yeah; the only difference is that they have more amenities today."

Realizing that I was not too keen in discussing the visit, my instructor changed the subject. He asked a few questions about the homeless shelter to which I provided very curt replies.

Riding along in silence for the rest of the way, my mind drifted between my two realities of prison and homelessness, both painful and both my truth, my lived experiences. The only saving grace for me about the visit was that I spent a few hours in prison without being an inmate.

CHAPTER 38
Convict Criminology: A Case Assessment

Completing the course work for the Masters degree, I had to make a decision whether to write a thesis or complete an internship. Not knowing what it would take to complete a thesis, I chose this option. I did so because I love reading, and wanted to improve my writing and research skills. To assist me with my project, I chose Dr P as my thesis director. Little did I realize what was in store for me when I made this decision.

The day I asked Dr. P to be the director of my thesis he did not say a word for about ten minutes. He got up from his desk, reached over to the stacks of books in his office and placed about fifteen of them on his desk. He then looked at me, smiled, and said, "If I am going to be your thesis director, you have to read these for starters. There are many more to come when you are finished with these." I looked at him and didn't know whether to laugh or balk. Recollecting from my momentary shock, I reached over and examined the books.

"Doc," I said somewhat reluctantly, "I don't see how these books relate to my thesis."

"Are you scared of reading?"

"No Doc, you know me better than that. You know I love to read."

"I know you love to read. Now, what is your problem? You know I will only supervise those who are willing to work."

"OK," I said. "I get the message," and gathered up the books.

The books my professor gave me to read included both academic and non-academic works. Among the five non-academic publications, two caught my attention almost immediately, *A Hope of the Unseen* by Suskind, and *Convicted in the Womb* by Carl Upchurch. I decided to read these first. Reading Suskind and Upchurch made me realize my professor's intention. Upchurch outlined the struggles of a young black man who moved from a life of delinquency and crime to imprisonment and reform. Suskind narrated the resilience of a young black kid who, despite the odds, succeeded in obtaining a college education.

As soon as I was finished reading these books, I went to my professor who said when he saw me with the books in my hands, "I see you get my message."

"What message?" I asked, pretending I didn't understand.

"Didn't you learn anything from Cedric?" he asked, referring to the main character in *A Hope of the Unseen*.

Unable to carry through with my pretence, I said, "Yes, I get it. Education does not come easily."

"Make sure you finish reading the other books and …," Before Dr. P could finish his sentence I asked, "What about my thesis? What am I going to do?"

"Finish the other books and then we will talk," he said. I was furious, but with tremendous effort restrained my anger.

It took about three months for me to finish reading the books and making detailed notes. Proud of my accomplishment, I approached Dr. P with my good news, "I am finished reading all the books," I announced with some glee. Without saying a word, Dr. P reached up into his bookshelf, pulled a book and tossed it over to me. "Take this, read and reread it. It will guide your thesis." I took a quick look at the book and upon reading the title smiled; it said *Convict Criminology*. The authors, Ross and Richards noted that the book presents and insiders (inmates) view of life behind bars. As they put it:

> [W]e were shocked by the number of criminologists who although they claim to be experts have little or no first hand experience with how human beings experience the criminal justice system. Whether it is because they have never worked in a prison, or in a police department, have been charged or convicted of a crime, or victimized by crime, the numbers are staggering. They simply do not comprehend the profound impact that imprisonment has on many individuals.

In an instant, I was hooked. Dr. P and I then talked a little about my thesis and we agreed that it should be my view of prison from the inside. We agreed on the title, *Convict Criminology: A Case Assessment.* "You knew this all along didn't you?" I asked. "Forget what I knew and didn't know, read the book," Dr. P answered. I was so happy with my topic, I began to read as soon as my conversation with Dr. P ended.

Before working on my thesis, I never gave much thought to my past, and especially my years as an inmate. I had kept detailed notes on various aspects of my life but never reread them. I knew I would like to write about my struggles one day which is why I kept notes. I never envisioned that these hand written notes of my past would one day become crucial in my pursuit of postsecondary education.

In guiding me on the thesis, Dr. P introduced me to the *Phenomenology of the Social World* by Alfred Schutz. Schutz' words became a source of comfort, and at time when I was down, they pulled me up. This is what Schutz said:

> The self-explication of my own lived experiences takes place within the total pattern of my experience. The total pattern is made up of meaning-contexts all my past lived experiences are at least present in me. They stand to a certain extent at my disposal, whether I see them once again in recognition or reproduction. We say in "free reproduction" because I can leave unnoticed any phases whatsoever and turn my attention to other phases previously unnoticed. In principle, however, the continuum which is my total stream of lived experience remains open in

its abundance at all times to my self-explication....
In summary it can be said that my own stream of
consciousness is given to me continuously in all its
fullness but yours is given to me in discontinuous
segments, never in its fullness, and only in "inter-
pretive perspectives."

I interpreted Schutz's comments to mean that I am the
most objective reporter of my lived experiences, and used
them as my guide in self analysis.

I can't recall how many times I stopped and cried while
writing my thesis. I know they were many. To recall my
past turned out to be more painful than I anticipated. But,
each time I cried, it seemed to have relieved me of some of
the burdens and pent up emotions I had carried around for
many, many years.

❦

CHAPTER 39
Graduation

My graduation blazer I bought at a thrift store. I had not worn a blazer in a long time, and was determined to attend the commencement ceremonies in style, albeit my own.

The day before graduation, I asked Dr. P if I could spend the night in his office. "I am going to receive my Masters degree and do not want to be late," I said to him. Recognizing my anxiety Dr. P said, "It's fine with me as long as campus security don't come in and kick you out."

At the end of the day, when everyone had left the building, I took my graduation clothes up to Dr. P's office, then went out to find something to eat. When I returned, I tried to read but could not concentrate. Looking out the glass walls of Dr. P's office, I could see students and their families walking around the campus. Some seemed in gay celebration already while others just walked around looking at the buildings and talking to each other. I could sense their anticipation as they gestured in excitement.

Across the street, a group of young men stood around drinking beers. From time to time they would erupt in laughter and slap each other five. They all seemed to be having a good time. I must have stared at the happenings on campus for almost an hour when suddenly the office went black. I waited a few minutes for the electricity to return but none of the lights came back on. Slowly, I opened the office door only to find that the entire building in darkness. At first, I thought someone had played a trick on me but after a half an hour or so, I realized there was a blackout. I closed the door, sat down in one chair, and pulled up another to rest my legs.

I must have dozed off for a while when the coldness of the office woke me up. Staring into the darkness, my thoughts started to drift. "I have come a long way," my mind echoed in silence, "I am going to receive my Masters degree; it was something I wanted to do just for me." As I wrestled with my addled mind, the thought struck that my education at FAMU was over. I had no place to go and no one with whom to share my moment of happiness. Suddenly, tears rolled down my cheeks as the new reality slowly dawned.

For most graduates, the Masters degree is a bridge into the future, a ticket for the ride on the pathway to success. I wish it was the same for me. With a Bachelors degree, I was on the lowest rung of the dishwashing crew, and with the Masters my status is not likely to change, unless someone sees value in me. In this land of plenty, in this land of opportunities, an ex-blue-collar-convict must bear his stigma of imprisonment for life. Denied opportunities to earn a living, he must face the future of bleakness with whatever resolve is left in him. As my thought drifted onto these realities, my eyes began to burn, and I slowly drifted in and out of sleep. In my loneliness, I found myself all alone.

I must have fallen into a deep sleep for about an hour when suddenly the electricity returned and awakened me. Realizing that day light would soon arrive, I read for a while then made a pot of coffee. I brushed my teeth, washed my face, and after a hot cup of coffee, got dressed and walked over to the football stadium where commencement ceremonies were scheduled to be held.

By the time I arrived at the stadium many students were already gathered there in jubilation. Accompanying them were members of their extended families who traveled from near and far to see their loved ones receive their degrees. Looking around, I saw young babies in their strollers, and elderly grandparents in their wheel chairs, all interacting in a beautiful display of familial bonding. For me, there would be no one in attendance, but I was still proud of my achievement. I've worked hard, and by the grace of God, and the assistance of several people, I was able to be among the graduating class of 2003.

Ushered into our designated seats, I began to scan the graduation booklet. To my surprise, among the several students to receive the Masters of Applied Social Science degree, I was the only one who had written a thesis. Upon discovering this fact, and seeing the title of my thesis in the booklet I smiled, and settled in my seat as the commencement ceremonies began.

Commencement speeches are forgotten soon after they are delivered. Mine was a little different. The speaker was television mogul Ted Turner. Turner made what would be considered a practical speech. It was not punctuated with philosophical statements, or what fine fellows we were and ready to conquer the world. Instead he talked about his displeasure with President Bush and the "War" in Iraq. He ended by promising every graduate - other than those with doctorate, pharmacy, or business degrees - a job at his new venture, "Ted's Montana Grill." All they had to do was to write and ask him for a job. In closing, he promised to shake everyone's hand and congratulate them personally. To me, this was monumental. I realized that not too many black people would get to shake hands with a "Billionaire" in their lifetime.

As Turner delivered his speech, I looked around at my graduating colleagues to see how many paid attention. Many were busy fanning themselves to prevent fainting under the blazing sun. In spite of the heat, no one complained about the university's decision to hold the commencement at the football stadium. The only complaints I heard was about the heat. From time to time students commented on something Turner said such "Montana grill Burgers." At the end of his speech, Turner received a thunderous applause, and a standing ovation from students.

Time came for announcing the names of the graduates; students turned to each other in chatter and excitement. With the announcement of each name came loud cheers and whistles from the graduating class. Looking into the crowded stadium, I could see people waving and hollering as their loved ones names' blared from loudspeakers located around the stadium. Names after names were announced with constant fanfare from all around. Then, after what seemed like an unending list of names, the announcer said, "Ulyses B. Hooks, Masters of Applied Social Sciences." I don't know if it was out of kindness or excitement, my graduation cohort cheered as I walked up to the stage. Several people were there to shake hands and congratulate students, among them stood Ted Turner.

As I reached out to shake Turner's hand, he said to me, "It's never too late." I guessed he said this because I obviously looked older than the other students, with my graying beard serving as a tattletale. Walking away I couldn't withhold my smile at the thought that crossed my mind: *The mogul and the homeless, two individuals from completely opposite existences clasped hands for a moment; both hands empty, mine always so; His? Rarely so.*

Leaving the stage, I rushed away in haste. There was no reason for me to hang around; I went to receive my diploma and did so. Walking through the crowd toward an exit, I heard someone calling out, "Ulyses ... Ulsyses wait ... Ulyses," I turned around to look, and there to congratulate me was Dr. P and Ms. Perkins. Once again, at a critical time in my life, my friends, instead of my family, showed up to support me and share my joy. Dr. P and Ms. Perkins had become my support system, my family away from my family. Being there to support me, I felt as if I was reliving my graduation experience from Bunker Hill Community College in Boston. Two people I had never known until I was in my forties showed up to wish me happiness, and congratulate me on my accomplishment. In Boston, Irene and her granddaughter were there to cheer me on when I received the Associates degree. They had become my family in Boston.

CHAPTER 40
A Journey Home To My Mother

After graduation, several people suggested that I pursue a doctorate degree. I decided to give it a try. Having some familiarity with Boston, I applied to the University of Massachusetts. Knowing that it would take several weeks for the university to process and respond to my application, I used the time to plan a visit to my mother. My mother had moved to Tustin, California. So, I began making preparations to go see her while awaiting the decision from the University of Massachusetts.

I am not sure what triggered my decision to visit my mother, but I knew that I needed to resolve some of the issues which led to our strained relationship. My indifference towards her did not happen overnight; it occurred incrementally over a prolonged period of time. Initially, I was too young to say anything to her. As I grew older, my indifference turned into resentment and my resentment into rebelliousness. Unable to address my frustrations and cope with my circumstances, I turned to alcohol as a form of escape and rebellion. This quickly led to the path of decadence and degradation. To this day, I still feel that my relationship with my mother helped to trigger my negativism that took me down the path of self destruction.

※ ※ ※

As I recall, this is what happened. My mother, while married to my father developed a relationship with one of my father's friend who sometimes visited her in my father's absence. Even as child, the relationship struck me as odd and disturbed me greatly. On a few occasions when the male friend visited, I confronted him. Being bigger than me, he would push me aside as my mother watched in silence. Because of his visits, the bonds and affection I had for my mother turned into mistrust. Too afraid to tell my father about the gentleman's visits, I turned my anger inward. Consumed by my internal misery, I began to rebel at school and soon this turned into a life of alcohol and drugs. Finally, my anger drove me to the point where I lost all semblances of rationality and control. Before I could figure out the cause of my degradation, I found myself driven deeper into a state of oblivion.

My mother probably never felt that her behavior troubled me. If she did, it was not manifested in any expressions of concern or care. As a child, her negligent behavior deeply affected me. She sought her own gratification, apparently without much thought of the impact on her family. Perhaps she felt her children lacked awareness, or were too naïve to understand the dynamics of her behaviors. But, in my view, children are territorial and sensitive, and can intuitively grasp any intrusions into their familial relationships.

It took years for me to realize that the manner in which some mothers live their lives may not be readily exemplified in their public personas. Yet, their behaviors do manifest themselves in their children's acts of rebelliousness, homelessness, drunkenness, drug addiction, prostitution, daring lifestyles or criminality. I grew up believing that even though a mother may innocently claim ignorance as to why her child is rebellious, she knows.

※ ※ ※

I arrived in Tustin, California in June 2004. My mother and her neighbor-landlord were at the bus station to pick me up. I had not seen her for nearly five years, and didn't know what to expect. Exhausted from the long bus ride, and years of struggle, I longed for a good rest. I greeted her hurriedly, jumped into the back seat of the car and we were on our way to her apartment. Throughout the drive we said very little. Given our prolonged separation, one would expect that a mother and her child would have a lot to talk about, but as I explained, my mother and I did not share a strong bond. What does a person say to a parent with whom he has had a strained relationship? I wish I knew. I felt like a stranger to my mother. We had grown so much apart, I did not did not know what to say or do in an attempt to improve and mend our relationship. I felt distant even though we shared the same space, and was always within speaking distance. Then, I remembered our phone conversations while I was away in graduate school. Occasionally, I called to see how she was doing so I used the same approach to start conversations with her. "Ma, how are you doing today?" I frequently started out. Then, we would talk about the news, her health and religion. Our conversations were always very short and innocuous.

Throughout my stay with my mother, I had very little appetite. Initially, I spent most of my time watching television, and sleeping. In the mornings, I would go to the mailbox hoping to hear from the University of Massachusetts. Each time I went, I came away empty handed. Then, irritability crept in. To pass the time, I became my mother's designated driver. She had recently gotten eye surgery which restricted her from driving. First, I undertook the task of driving her back and forth to the doctor. It was like taking the driving test with a police officer from the department of motor vehicles. "Watch out Junior, turn here Junior, you going too fast Junior," These were her mantra. In a few days, however, I passed her driving test, and became accepted as her designated driver. From then on, we went everywhere, to Wal-Mart, the grocery store, the bank, to pay various bills, and wherever else that she felt like going. If there was a script on how to be a son, I needed it because I never truly learned how to be one.

CHAPTER 41
Back On The Road To Homelessness

M y stay at my mother's house was quickly coming to a close. The apartment in which she lived was governed by section eight housing policies that restricted the length of time a family member could stay with her. I had overextended my time and knew I had to move. I called Dr. P and asked him to send me a bus ticket to Clearwater, Florida. I chose Clearwater because my younger brother who lives there had said that I could call on him if I needed assistance. I also called another friend, Ms. Taylor, a librarian at Florida A. & M. University who promised to send me a few dollars for expenses. I was ready to leave my mother's apartment, but was also anxious to hear from the University of Massachusetts's regarding my application to the gerontology PhD. Program.

Tired of waiting on the University of Massachusetts officials to contact me, I contacted them. The person with whom I spoke informed me that I was denied admission, and that she sent a letter regarding the decision to my FAMU address. According to my calculations the letter was sent out ten-days before I left Florida for California. It was sent to The School of Graduate Studies at Florida A. & M. University as per my instructions. For some reason I never received the letter. The denial of admission into the PhD, program disappointed me, but I had to pick up the pieces and move on.

The bus ticket from Dr. P arrived just in time for me to change my life and environment, and shortened the time to dwell on my loss. The day of my departure, my mother and her landlord-neighbor took me to the bus station. I had mixed feelings leaving because I did not know what lay ahead. Actually, I did not have a specific destination, just somewhere in Clearwater, Florida, near to where my brother lives.

Once again, the long bus ride gave me time to pause in reflection. Except for the time spent in seeking an education, I seem to lack stability. Homeless before going to college, homeless during college, I was once again thrust into homelessness after my college education. I moved from a homeless individual without a degree to a homeless with a degree. My education did not elevate or improve my homeless status. It did, however, enable me to critically assess my life. In some respects I have failed, and in others, I have succeeded. But, success did not bring improvements in my material circumstances. As these things run through my mind, I searched the distance from my bus window, and thanked the Lord that I was still alive.

When I arrived in Clearwater, Florida, I went downtown in search of the Salvation Army to secure a place to stay for the night. I found the building after asking directions from passersby. To my disappointment, the doors were closed. A sign on it instructed people to go to the St. Petersburg, Florida branch of the Salvation Army where they would be accommodated. Without an alternative place to stay, I took the city bus from Clearwater to St. Petersburg.

The Salvation Army at St. Petersburg, housed in a fairly new building, seemed well kept. After being interviewed by the attendant, I received a three night stay with the possibility of an extension, if I could provide a valid reason. I was quite pleased with the dorm room assigned to me. Immaculately kept, it felt pleasant, and had its own shower and bath. Each individual had a bed with a clean sheet, pillowcase and a blanket. Excited about the accommodation, I explained my circumstances to a counselor the next day after breakfast. She listened and granted me a thirty-day stay so that I could look for a job.

Seeking employment after being in prison, homeless and in college, are not the kinds of experiences someone puts on a resume. And, since potential employers consider experience to be a major pre-requisite for employment, my prospect for obtaining a job seemed remote at best. In looking for a job, my search would frequently come to an abrupt end with the question, "What kind of experience do you have?" Sometimes I felt like saying, "I was a model prisoner, or I was the best dishwasher in town," but held my response so as not to offend anyone. I went to several drug rehabilitation programs, homeless shelters, and the Urban League. All denied me employment for one reason or another. It seemed that I was more educated than many of the employees, and they became somewhat suspicious.

Every evening, upon my return to the Salvation Army, I would reassess my day's employment search. Each time I did, I found myself grappling with some of the same sort of issues touched on by Ross and Richards in their book on *Convict Criminology*. Is the prison system best understood by someone who has had minimal contact with it, or never know what's it like from the inside? Can someone address the issues of the homeless who has never experienced homelessness, but simply observed the homeless from a distance? Can someone really address how it feels to be an alcoholic and drug addict if he never experienced the effects of these substances? I have seen and experienced prison, homelessness and addiction as an outsider and insider. Yet I was not qualified for employment in any of these areas. As Dr. P remarked factiously from time to time during the writing of my thesis, "Remember Ulyses, the best child psychologist never raised a child, and the best marriage counselor never lived with a spouse."

As a last resort, I went to St. Petersburg College with the hope of finding some sort of work there. After speaking with the provost, I showed her my Master's degree from FAMU. She looked at it as if it came from some foreign institution she never heard of before. Sensing her discomfort, I jokingly asked her if she would accept my diploma in exchange for a bus ticket back to Tallahassee. She politely refused. That evening, I called my mother, and she wired me enough money to get back to Tallahassee.

People on the FAMU campus seemed shocked to see me back in Tallahassee. In my mind, this is where I belonged. I received my postsecondary education here, and was very familiar with the surroundings. It would be easy for me to plan my next move, I surmised.

The first thing I did upon arriving on the FAMU campus was to contact Dr. Haywood, - the Dean of Graduate Studies. I asked for her help in trying to get a position on campus. She told me to give her a couple of days to get in touch with her colleagues to see what was available. She also mentioned that some faculty members had received a grant-award of four million dollars to conduct research in Gerontology, and that I may be able to work with the group. When she said Gerontology a light went off in my head. I had just applied for the PhD Program in Gerontology at the University of Massachusetts, Boston. The position paper I submitted as part of my application package had some ideas on the gerontology of the homeless and prison populations. I had discussed some of these ideas over the phone with my contact in Boston. Now, I would be able to explore some of my ideas, if I succeeded in getting a position with the research group. In less than a week, my hopes were dashed. Dr. Haywood sent me an e-mail to let me know that all of the positions in gerontology had been filled.

Once again I reached a dead end. I hung around Dr. P's office running errands for Dr. Dix-Richardson, Ms. Perkins, and Dr. P. People kept suggesting that I continue in my efforts to gain admission into a PhD. Program. One day, I decided to go to Washington, D.C, and apply to Howard University. Reverend Ivy Williams, my spiritual and financial support at the time, purchased a ticket for me to get to Washington, D.C. A few days later, I left for D.C.

CHAPTER 42
Rejected By Howard University

I first heard of Howard University in the late seventies while serving time in the Oklahoma State Penitentiary. About to be released, I applied to Howard for admission. I had read a lot in prison which heightened my consciousness regarding minorities and other disadvantaged groups. At the time, Howard University seemed to be in the forefront of the struggle for social change. Radical students at the institution took to the streets, demonstrating against racism and oppression.

The application materials I received from Howard University awakened my lust for postsecondary education. A brochure entitled "Black Fire," depicted black people, young and old, sitting around the reflecting pool at the "Lincoln" memorial in Washington, D.C. With their shoes and sneakers off, they sat cooling their feet in the water after their march with Dr. Martin Luther King Jr. The picture turned out to be the most powerful depiction of the march I had ever seen in my life. It was as if Howard University was saying to me, "Come my down-trodden brother. If you can overcome the trials and tribulations to get here, we will welcome you, and help you pick up the pieces." From that moment, I knew I had to travel to Washington, D.C, in whatever condition, and by any means necessary. Once there, I felt I would be allowed to get an education.

ﰈ ﰈ ﰈ

The opportunity for me to go to D.C., came when my younger brother Craig called and suggested that I move there and live with him and his wife after my release from prison. Given my mental and physical state at the time, I was not prepared for college, and pushed Howard University out of my mind. I did, however, visit the university.

In 1979, during homecoming, I accompanied my ex-wife to hear Imamu Amiri Baraka speak. Before the show started, I took my ex-wife backstage to see Baraka. I had written a play I wanted him to review. Away from the audience, behind the screens, Baraka stored all the Heineken beers he bought for his crew from a small café in the area. He offered me a Heineken beer. I took it, and handed him a copy of my play. He said that he would review it and send it back. A few weeks later he did send the play back with no fanfare.

On another occasion, I went to see Sterling Brown (the poet) at Founders Library on Howard's campus. He had a small office on the top floor where they kept the African American collection. I didn't know it at the time but his wife had just died, and he was in mourning. I waited for some time, knocked on his door, and then opened it. Sterling Brown sat in a bent position over his desk. A young black female student played old thirty three records of Billie Holiday moaning some tune. Peering at me as I entered the office, Brown asked what I wanted. I told him I wanted him to look at my play. He screamed at me saying, "I can't even look at my own work; how can I look at yours?" Disappointed and hurt, I left him to his sorrow.

※ ※ ※

The Greyhound bus pulled into the crowded D.C., station. Once again I arrived in the nation's capital not knowing where I would live. I last visited the city with a friend in the late nineties during my Spring break. Now, in 2004, it had changed considerably. It was late at night. The only people up and about were the homeless. I walked the streets looking for shelter in the old familiar places, but didn't find any. Exhausted, I asked a policeman on Second and D, Street N.W, where I could find shelter. He gave me the run around. Eventually, I located a drop-in shelter, went in, and after undergoing the third degree by the night attendant, crawled onto the floor and went to sleep.

For a couple of nights I slept in various drop-in shelters trying to figure out how to execute my plan for graduate school at Howard University. I knew that it would not be easy, but life had never been easy for me. I was determined to get into a PhD, Program at Howard University.

One morning, I left a drop-in shelter in the "Mount Pleasant" neighborhood of D.C, and walked down Columbia Road. Passing by a Safeway grocery store, I suddenly remembered that I had a food stamp card that I obtained while in Saint Petersburg, Florida. I went into the grocery store and asked a cashier if she could check to see how much cash allowance I had remaining on the card. It had one hundred and forty nine dollars. It wouldn't take a "Rocket Scientist" to figure out my next decision. I went into the deli section and ordered a custom sub. With sub, soda and chips in hand, I left the store to find a quiet place to eat. Finally, I decided on "Logan Circle" park. I was familiar with the area since I had lived a block away from the park, on 12th and R. Street some twenty years before. After eating my sandwich I walked to Howard University to begin the long process of applying for the PhD.

Walking down Vermont Avenue to 12th and R. Street, I recognized a house where I once lived. I decided to go in and inquire if Reverend Carter stilled lived there. The gate in the front yard was open, so I went up onto the porch and looked into the window. Knocking on the door and ringing the bell brought no response. I was about to leave when a middle-aged man showed up. I asked him if Reverend Carter lived there and he said, "Yes. Come on up. I'll take you to her."

Reverend Carter, close to eighty years of age, was sitting in a wheel chair when I walked in. Her eyes lit up when she saw me. "I was just thinking about you," she said. Her words brought me some comfort, and we began to talk. She told me that she had fallen down some time back, and had to have hip surgery. This left her partially disabled. Other than that, she said she felt fine, and that everything was okay. She went on to say that she had sold her house, and would have to be out of it by March 2005. Meanwhile, she had taken on some boarders, three of whom did not pay any rent.

Her only paying renter was a Harvard law school graduate who suffered from some type of stress disorder, and was on medication. A sister of the reverend also lived with her. They both shared the living room as their residential quarter. Looking around the room, I saw several empty meals on wheels containers. A mountain of letters filled their bed. I would later spend days helping the reverend sort through her bed-full of mails.

I explained my situation to Reverend Carter, and why I had journeyed back to Washington, D.C. We both felt that it was not a coincidence that our paths had crossed again. It was as though my soul had led me there. I also explained to her that I had about one hundred and forty dollars on my food stamp card, and that I would be willing to buy her one hundred dollars worth of groceries each month, as a way to compensate her for allowing me to stay in her basement. She agreed, and told me to go downstairs and find me a spot.

For the next few months I slept on the basement floor. Some nights the extreme cold made me miserable, but I did not complain. Residing in the basement was better than being out on the streets. After buying the Reverend Carter a hundred dollars worth of food, I used the remaining forty dollars worth of food stamps to feed myself. I made it a point to never to eat any of her food because I did not want to be accused of trying to take advantage of her. After a few days doing nothing in particular, I went out to make investigations into the possibilities of enrolling in graduate school.

On reflection, I recalled that Father Sloan, the rector at Saint Paul's Episcopal Church, had told me to look him up whenever I got back to Washington, D.C. I last contacted him from St. Petersburg, Florida, requesting that he send a copy of my baptismal certificate to a church there from which I was seeking assistance. Now in D.C, I thought it best to call on Father Sloan. I considered him my best resource in the area. Father Sloan had baptized me at St. Paul's on Easter Sunday, and members of his congregation had helped me to start over. I may have let them down by falling by the wayside again; but, how was I to know in my "substance abusive" state of mind. The pain and anguish of failure impacted my core, and disappointed church members. Now, I felt the situation was different. I was returning to the church a college graduate with a master's degree, not as a homeless drug and alcohol addict.

I rang the church rectory's door bell and an elderly white female assistant welcomed me into the foyer. I told her I had an appointment to see father Sloan. After waiting about fifteen minutes I was called into his office. I took a seat and began to tell father Sloan about my journey. I told him that I was there to apply to Howard University's PhD, Program in Sociology. He informed me that he didn't have any money, and suggested that I go to a church which they supported. The church, he said, has a program that assists needy people in obtaining jobs. I felt as if Father Sloan hadn't listened to anything I said. I was crushed. Simply put, the church would not support me. I thanked him, shook his hand, and left.The reality of how hard it is to accomplish a goal without any resources hit me like a ton of bricks. It was a set back, but not a total defeat. Without having any resources of my own, I was still able to finish the Masters degree. I was not going to quit. These thoughts filled my mind as I climbed the steps to the building that housed the Sociology Department at Howard University. I decided that maybe if I get to know the professors in the department, and let them get to know me, I might have a chance to pursue the PhD.

Walking through the hallway, I happened to see Dr. Ralph Gomes, Director of Graduate Studies of Sociology and Anthropology. He was sitting in his office. I interrupted him, and went in. Without going into much detail, I gave him a quick history of myself, pointing out that I had to overcome a host of obstacles to get an education. I also explained that I wanted a chance to prove myself at the PhD level, and that I had applied to the University of Massachusetts gerontology program without success. During the conversation, Dr. Gomes seemed only partially interested in what I had to say. Upon hearing that the University of Massachusetts rejected my application for admission, he became openly impatient, and seemed in a hurry to shoo me from his office. He indicated that the office of Graduate Studies handled all applications, and that if I was interested in their program, to sign up, and the staff would forward my application to him for review. I left his office feeling demoralized at such callousness by a dean of Howard University. Afterwards, it seemed that everywhere I went on campus, people looked at me as if to say, "What are you doing here? We don't need people like you." The negative feelings stayed with me throughout my days in D.C.

Winter came, and D.C, was getting very cold. For several days I walked to Howard University to check on the progress of my application. It had become a test of will to brave the weather, and to face the unfriendly attitudes of the people at Howard University. When I started the application process the ladies in the Graduate Studies office greeted me in a "what do you want" manner. And, after frequent visits to check on the status of my application, they told me that I did not have to frequent the office, "You will be informed of the decision when it is made," they said. Determined to make sure that they process my application, I kept showing up, much to the annoyance of the office staff.

Once when I showed up, the graduate studies staff told me that they were awaiting my Graduate Record Examination scores. Knowing that I had not scored well on the exam, the thought entered my mind that they might refuse me admission into the PhD, Sociology program. It had never dawned on me that a Historically Black University would not accept me. I had the proper credentials and I was black. "Weren't Black colleges created to give Black people like me a chance to acquire higher education?" I questioned no one in particular.

CHAPTER 43
Reconnecting With Angel Tina and Meeting My Daughter

Rejected almost everywhere I turned to for assistance, I decided to contact Tina one of my former D. C., church members whom I trust. A kind and gentle lady, Tina worked for a museum in D.C. I first came in contact with her in the 80's. At that time she fed Washington, D.C's, street people early in the mornings. And, she also assisted them in other ways whenever she could. Tina still helps the poor today.

Tina lived in an apartment adjacent to the church with her roommate Michael. One day, with little hope left, I knocked on Tina's door. Excitedly, she greeted me with a hug, and invited me in. Sitting around her kitchen table, we drank coffee and ate cheese and crackers, while talking about old times. On the visit, I took with me my framed Bachelor of Science degree to leave with for safekeeping. After explaining my situation, Tina packed an assortment of canned soup for me to take. She also gave me a couple of dollars. I gratefully took the gifts and went on my way. I would come to rely on her generosity again before leaving D.C.

For many D.C.'s homeless, Tina was truly an *Angel*. She braved all types of weather to go out and feed them. I have never seen someone who cared so intensely for the downtrodden and the dehumanized, those who many considered as society's rejects. To learn that Tina still fed the homeless was very heartening, and I took great pride in knowing her. She could have turned her back on me when I knocked on her door. Instead, she greeted me warmly, shared her coffee with me, and listened to my lament. She never imposed her solution on me by telling me what I could or should have done. She simply listened, empathized and wished me well. When I left her apartment that day, I kept thinking how few people like Tina in the world today.

The holiday season came around and filled me with sadness. I had not spent Christmas in a family setting in about ten years. The people around me seemed to be enjoying the festivities, but I could not get into the holiday spirit. My family members, scattered in many parts of the country, have become estranged after years of prolonged separation. All I had left were the memories of my youth. Oh! How my brothers, sisters and I jumped around and frolicked during the Christmas season. Our lives erupted with glee and anticipation. The merriment of children stormed our neighborhood as Christmas carols from neighbors' stereos filled the atmosphere. It was truly beautiful then. Now, all I have is the memories; they have become the treasures of my youthful past. Without doubt, aging is a painful process to a homeless man.

Right after Christmas my daughter called Reverend Carter and asked for directions on how to get to her house. She wanted to meet with me. I had tried to contact her when I arrived in D.C, but was unsuccessful. I hadn't seen her in twenty years, so I didn't know what to expect from her visit. My last memories of her were from the 80's when I pushed her around in a baby stroller. I would stop at the corner convenience stores and replenish my sixteen-ounce cans of *Old English 800*, malt liquor and tour D.C., with her. People often complimented me about her beauty as we stood on the subway platform waiting for the train. On one occasion we stayed out until dark. It alarmed her mother so much she stood in the front yard waiting on us to get home. That was then. What would my daughter think of me now; a fifty eight old man sleeping in a basement, penniless, homeless, jobless, but still chasing a lofty dream?

As soon as daughter entered through the door and walked into the room, my eyes gave her the "once over" to see if there was a resemblance to me. She was beautiful. I could hardly imagine that I had held her in my arms when she was a baby. She looked me up and down and said, "Finally I meet my other half." My mind raced, reminding me repeatedly that this was the chance encounter I had dreamt about; I could say all of the things I wanted to say to her for so long, but I was afraid to speak. Momentarily speechless, I tried desperately to restrain my emotions and withhold my tears. Standing before me was my own daughter, a precious young lady to whom I was hardly a father.

Despite being her father, I had done little to nurture my daughter. Her mother had relieved me of that duty. I had protested in vain. But who was I to protest? I lacked stability and the sense of responsibility. Now, with my daughter before me, I could make no claims. For a while we talked about her education and her future plans. She did attend a few colleges, but did not stay long enough to graduate. She explained that she was interested in the fashion industry. "Learning the craft of fashion you would have to put in some hard times," I told her. "As a beginner, you will have to start from the bottom, and it is not all that glamorous." I am not sure how she took my words for she showed little emotion.

We ended the reunion with me telling her that I was determined to get my PhD, if not at Howard University, somewhere else. For some unknown reason, I asked her if she had she been molested. She avoided the question. I walked her to her car, kissed her on the jaw, and waved goodbye as she drove off. We have not communicated since that day, but memories of her are etched deeply in my heart. I was happy that she did have the courage to visit me. Now, I no longer have to imagine what she looks like. Whenever I want to see her beautiful face I can now access it from my aging memory bank. Oh! How comforting her image is to my tortured Soul.

January came around. It grew colder. By the middle of the month, it snowed heavily. I decided to seek new lodging because the time was near for the new owners to take possession of the house from Reverend Carter. It wasn't hard for me to get admitted into the Community for Creative Non-Violence Shelter on Second and D. Street. I called the staff on duty, explained my situation, and he accepted me into the shelter. That night I took a long hot shower, and slept in a bed, with sheets, a pillow, and a blanket. It felt good to get off of the floor, and out of Reverend Carter's cold basement.

The next day I underwent the shelter's intake process. The counselor asked me for my social security card and a picture identification which I provided to him. He then questioned me about my aspirations and plans for the future. Already frustrated with my circumstances, his questioning annoyed me. I told him that I was there because of my circumstances and not because he worked there. When I told him that I had applied for a PhD. program at Howard University, he stared at me with such suspicion that his face betrayed his doubt. He gave me a list of mandatory things that I would have to do. It included applying for public housing, getting food stamps, and taking a tuberculosis test. With all of these things completed, he informed me that I would be monitored and evaluated on a random basis to determine my progress. I signed all of the papers, and verbally agreed to the rules. Thus, I became a member of the community, at least for a short while.

It was a long walk from the shelter to Howard University, but I made the daily trek. I spent most of my time in the university's Founders library using the Internet and checking my e-mails. Given my unkempt physical state, I felt as if everyone focused their eyes on me when I sat at the computer. When people laughed, I wondered if they were laughing at me or because, somehow, they knew I was homeless. Did they consider me a fool for pursuing my goal? The word homeless had become painful. No longer a carefree reckless youth, the word pricked at my conscience. Something inside of me cringed when I heard people talk about the homeless. In spite of the perception, I knew I had to forge ahead. I could not abandon my goal by running away and hide. There I was, waiting, hoping, dreaming; about what? - About the American dream, and a future with some modicum of success. But, the opposition had always proven to be stronger, thus in my efforts, I failed.

I started my homeless journey long ago, and in the process sought to attain a college education. To date, my struggles proved very painful. No other human should have to suffer the same. Some people know not what they do, or do they? I kept hoping that if it was meant for me to be admitted to Howard University, it would happen. Had I not suffered enough? Many times my Soul cried out for mercy, but eyes did not see any glory, and my mind retracted in pain.

At one point I felt swallowed up into the darkness of the universe. I had journeyed into the dark abyss. There was no one, or nothing left, for me to rely on. In the past, I had called on God, but man always pretended to be more powerful. What had I done to forfeit the aid of God? Was it predestined that I should lose? What danger did I pose to the workings of society? These questions goad at my sub-conscious as I made my way to Howard University's School of Graduate Studies one day.

The lady in the graduate studies office looked up at me as soon as I walked through the door. Before I reached her desk she said without looking straight at me, "They have not made a decision on your application as of yet. Your application is the last to be reviewed." For a moment, I stood there stunned by her remarks. I was among the first applicant for the Fall Semester. How could it be that I was the last to be reviewed? On my way out of her office I told the lady that I was tired of being last, and that one day I would prove to be a thorn in her side.

The following day I went to see Dr. Ralph Gomes, Director of Graduate Studies for the Department of Sociology and Anthropology. He told me that he was unable to grant me admission because of my academic background and interest. After talking with me, he concluded that I would be better suited for the PhD. program in Social Work. How Dr. Gomes come to such a conclusion still baffles me. I earned a Bachelors degree in Sociology, and a Masters degree in Criminal Justice. I never studied Social Work or took even a single course in the field. As if to get rid of me, Dr. Gomes wrote me a note to take to the School of Social Work. I guess that it was his way of saying, "good riddance".

At the school of Social Work, a female staff told me that I had to have a master's degree in Social Work to be eligible for admission into the PhD program. The tone in the lady's voice indicated clearly that she did not want me in her program either. Whether Gomes called her to alert her to my visit, I do not know. The unfolding events, however, appeared quite suspicious. I left the lady's office defeated. My parting words to her were, "I'll see you in court." Coming from a homeless man without a dime my parting threat now seems quite humorous.

The next morning I went to the Department of Education, intent on seeing someone to lodge a complaint about the unethical treatment I received from officials at Howard University. I got as far as the lobby. The guard at the reception desk took my name and called a number. When she hung up the phone, she gave me a couple of telephone numbers to call. I stood there and dialed all the numbers but no one answered. At that point I realized that I had reached a dead end. I was a homeless black man at the Department of Education in Washington, D.C, trying to lodge a complaint of unfair treatment against an educational institution which claimed to support Blacks. It seemed so absurd. On my way out, I told the guard to tell Howard University that I would take them to court. I knew it was useless verbiage.

Walking away from the Department of Education, I realized that Black people had denied me. They didn't even want to talk to me. Is this Black life in America? Black people were now doing to black people what white people had done to them in the past, "Black faces, White minds." "This is how a Black man must have felt as white people carried him off to be hung," I mumbled to myself. No one was around to save me.

A few days after my ordeal with Howard University and the Department of Education, I became uneasy in D.C. What if they felt I had made threats to Howard officials? With emotions running high in the nation's capital regarding threats, I started to conjure images of harassment by the law enforcement authority. Even though I didn't threaten anyone physically, who could predict what will happen, given the paranoia that prevailed in D.C. Afraid of being harassed and jailed, I decided to leave the city. I called Dr. P at FAMU, and told him I needed a ticket back to Tallahassee. He said he would see what he could do.

When I spoke to Dr. P, he said that an F.B.I. agent had visited him to gather information on a former student. He also said that he told the agent that he had a student in a

Washington homeless shelter who needed a bus ticket, and if he would be kind enough to take the ticket to him. He laughed saying that the agent informed him that it was against the bureau's policy to do such a favor. Nevertheless, I gave him the address to my church, and he promised to send a ticket, or the money to get one within a few days.

After three days, I went to the church to check on Dr. P's letter. Tina happened to be there. I told her that I was leaving town and that I would need to pick up the diploma I had given her for safe keeping. The letter from Dr. P did arrive. I took the letter from the church assistant and talked for a while about how things didn't always happen the way a person anticipated, but that a person must carry on. Later, I picked up my degree, thanked Tina for helping me, and told her goodbye.

I went to the bus station and purchased a seven day advanced ticket to Tallahassee, Florida. That was the easy part. Now I had to live in the Community for Creative Non-Violence shelter for seven more days. This was the hard part. Unlike in my youth, I found it difficult to be in a shelter full of black men who were reduced to nothing. Sadly, they thought that they were 'getting over' on the system. They paraded around in nice clothes, talking on their cell phones, and being pampered by a number of church organizations that fed them food continuously. From anywhere in the building, you would hear them say from time to time, "They're feeding outside." The words rang out as a cry of joy, and not of pain. On some days, groups of students received tours through the building as if the place was a "human zoo." Maybe the anthropologist Desmond Morris was correct that "Human Zoos" do exist. At this particular D.C, shelter it seemed as if the tamed homeless were on display for students to observe.

Overanxious to wait the required six days for the validation of my bus ticket, I decided to go to the bus station and inquire if I could leave early. For some reason my luck prevailed. I was allowed to board the bus late Wednesday night. I was on my way back to Tallahassee, Florida. Thanks to Dr. P. In D.C, I learned about the plight of an ex-convict, drug addict, alcoholic, homeless person trying to accomplish his goals and realize his dreams in America. In some respects I failed in my pursuit, not because of my lack of ability, but because of the lies inherent in the American system regarding justice and equality for all.

CHAPTER 45
Homeless In Tallahassee

B ack in Tallahassee, I began again to assist Dr. Dix, Ms. Perkins and Dr. P with various tasks. All of them had welcomed me back with open arms. They made me feel at home in their company. I called my sister in Oklahoma to let her know that I arrived safely, and that I could be contacted by way of Dr. P. She seemed pleased. I also walked around the campus to renew contacts with my few friends, and letting them know of my unsuccessful attempt in gaining admission to Howard University.

Unsure of what to do next, I began reading voraciously on varied topics. Mostly, I read sociology, literature, philosophy and the daily newspapers. Regularly, I tried to entertain undergraduate students in discourses on current affairs. Not too many seemed interested. Some didn't even know what I was talking about, even though the issues appeared in the daily newspapers. I can't say they discouraged me by their lack of interest. Instead, I used the opportunity to encourage them to read. After a while some started to listen, and visited me while I sat in Dr. P's office reading.

Dr. P's office serves more than a sanctum for my homeless soul. It is there that I take my morning coffee, and eat my microwave meals. Over the decades of hardships, I have gotten accustomed to eating very little. Some times Dr. P would take me to lunch. I introduced him to Churches fried chicken because it was cheap. After going to Churches a few times he said to me one day, "Ulyses, promise me you won't ask to go there again." From the way he said it I knew he was disgusted. "What happen, you don't like the place?" I asked. He looked at me quizzically without providing an answer. I got the message.

On occasions Dr. P and I would walk to the supermarket located some three quarters of a mile from campus, to pick up munchies which he keeps in his office. I hated the walk and complained a lot. "You need the exercise Ulyses. Come on, don't be lazy. You need to clean those congested lungs you polluted for so many years," Dr. P would say. On these trips to the supermarket, Dr. P and I talked a lot, mostly about politics and me. Talking to him gave me the opportunity to purge my mind which became overburdened by decades of suffering. Once he asked if living in the homeless shelter was painful for me. "Of course it is painful Doc. One day I hope I can afford an apartment of my own." Dr. P looked at me in usual silence.

In an attempt to assist me in finding employment, Dr. P and Dr. Dix suggested that I apply to be an adjunct professor within FAMU's department of Sociology and Criminal Justice. Reluctant at first, I filled out the application and provided all supporting documentation to the department chairperson. Within two weeks, the department head notified me that I was scheduled to teach two juvenile justices courses, the Social Problems of Youth, and Youth Management and Community Organization, starting in the 2005 Fall, semester. In anticipation of the start of classes, I prepared my syllabi, and began reading widely on the subject area. I asked Dr. P if using my lived experiences as a youth would be acceptable. "Ulyses," he said, "you are better prepared than anyone else I know to teach these courses. You will bring to the classroom tangible evidence of the problems that afflict many African American youths today."

"Doc, you're not putting me on, are you?" I responded.

"No Ulyses. You know I am the one who used to teach those courses. I can talk of being arrested, but I don't know what it feels like, you do. I can talk about being suspended from school, but do I know the humiliation and degradation that accompany it? Of course not; you do."

"Come on Doc, are you trying to insult me or something?"

"Why would I do that Ulyses?"

"I don't know Doc? I know you are not, but just the sound of it."

"I am not trying to insult you in any way. Your presentations of some of the problems such as detachment from the family, arrests, drug use etc., will have the emotional sincerity that only those who suffer such can articulate them convincingly."

After listening to Dr. P, I felt reassured that I would be an effective instructor. From then on, I began to plan mentally and physically how I would instruct my class.

Close to the start of the semester, I received a call from the head of department. "Ulyses can you come over to my office, I need to talk to you," he said. I left what I was doing and rushed over to see him. As soon as I reached the door of his office, he said, "I am sorry, you won't be able to teach." I told him thanks and left.

Back in Dr. P's office, I kept wondering about the rejection. I had provided FAMU with all my documentation, transcripts, letters of recommendation, driver's license etc., and signed the necessary employment papers. Why the sudden denial. I kept thinking that it could be because of my prison history. But, my past record of arrests is known. Furthermore, it is well documented in my Masters thesis. If university officials were concerned about my past they could have informed me about it before signing the employment offer. They need not have waited until the first week of school to inform me that I was considered ineligible for employment. Extremely disappointed, I did my best to hide my emotional state.

FAMU would not have made history had they hired me, an ex-convict, to teach. Many colleges and universities have ex-convicts within their faculty ranks. And these individuals have contributed immensely to the criminal justice field. Richard Jones, Stephen Richards, Charles Terry and Edward Tromanhauser have all served time in prison. Not only have these men become faculty members at various universities, they have made significant contributions to the field of criminal justice with their insiders' assessments of prisons. As I reflected on the lives of these professors, I couldn't help but think of the many students who benefited from them.

Since attending FAMU, I have always used my past history to deter students from a life of crime. Teaching would have allowed me to reach a wider audience of students, not only to influence them away from criminal activities, but also to train them to become better mentors to at risk youths. I have lived and suffered the consequences of being a problem youth. I have regretted my past, and my future has already passed on by. Am I not a prime example of what happens to someone with a criminal past? If I am not, then who is? I am haunted by my past, ashamed of my present and afraid about my future. In fact, what is my future when my past has contaminated my present? And, my present, which leads into the future, is already darkened with hopelessness and degradation? Each day I live in fear of the future. I do not see how the lives of today's at-risk youths will be better than mine, if they do not receive proper guidance. Will they too live in fear of the future, or are they already doing so?

CHAPTER 46
Is There My Tomorrow?

For most of my adult life I have had to struggle with the pains of homelessness. Some may say that I deserve the consequences, that being homeless is my own fault. They are right. I have no one to blame but myself. But how was I to know? Like so many minority kids of my generation, I was caught up in a different world, one in which there was no future, no hope. To escape a life of decadence, many of my peers joined the military. I tried to follow suit, but the military rejected me.

Prosecuted by the justice system for a crime I didn't commit filled me with resentment and compounded my problems. I lost faith, and felt driven into a state of hopelessness in which there was no return. Everywhere I looked, my future seemed bleak. Caught in a downward spiral, I lacked the strength and the will to extricate myself. I traveled down the road to destruction fast. Drugs and alcohol consumed me as quickly I consumed them.

As the years passed, and I sobered up, I began to take a more critical look at myself. In retrospect, I could see clearly where I could have done things differently. Retrospection, however, is an exact science of days and incidences gone by. It does not provide answers into the future. Looming larger than retrospection is aging. Growing old, forces one to think both retrospectively and prospectively. Through prospective thinking, the frailty of the human specie comes toward you with all its force. The questions of Spirituality ring thunderously in the psyche, and torment the living Soul. Yes, the pompousness of youth defiles the Spirit. But, how does one come to know that such is occurring? Is there a Spiritual plan outlined for each and every one of us? If so, how does it manifest itself to the human kind? Many nights I laid awake appealing to the Supreme for answers to my tortured Soul. Many nights I bent my knees in prayer seeking Divine intervention to my current plight. Whether anyone listened or heard my pleas, I do not know. I am still here, alone and peering into the darkness of my homeless existence.

Today, the Tallahassee homeless shelter still serves as my home. Each evening, as I walk to the shelter, my heart sinks a little more for I am not sure how many more nights I will have to sleep there, or where my journey will end. Some nights, I would lay awake thinking of my life, and of my daughter. I have failed her as a father. In my younger days, I did not think often of her. I was lost. Now that I am older, I can't get her out of my mind. Does she think of me as often as I think of her? The last time I saw her in Washington D.C, I wanted to hug her and never let go. I wanted to tell her how much I love her, and that I am sorry I was never there for her. My life was in disarray, and still is. I was, and still am, homeless and disenfranchised. My daughter does not need my burden. I wish I could be with her, not as an appendage but as a provider. Because of my advanced age and past history, I am of little value to anyone. I still dream of being self sufficient, and having a simple apartment to call my home. Perhaps my dream is too lofty, but then again, there may be one *Guardian Angel* left in my homeless path. Only God knows. For now, it seems that all I have left is to wait my turn for the Precious Lord to take my hand and lead me home to the place without homelessness.

BIOGRAPHICAL SKETCH

NARAYAN PERSAUD is an Associate Professor at Florida A & M University where he teaches courses in Criminal Justice and Sociology. He earned his PhD. from Florida State University and serves as an adjunct professor at this institution. He has published several journal articles and a monograph entitled *Mentoring With A Humane Face*, published by Thomson Publishing.

ULYSES B. HOOKS JR. holds an Associate Degree from Bunker Hill Community College in Boston Massachusetts, and Bachelors and Masters' degrees from Florida A & M University. He served two terms in prison. The first lasted two and half years, and the second, six and half years. In 1979 he was discharged from prison and never returned. From the early age of eighteen he drifted in and out of homeless.

CPSIA information can be obtained
at www.ICGtesting.com
Printed in the USA
FFHW021036200919
55113626-60815FF